# teacher's friend
# publications

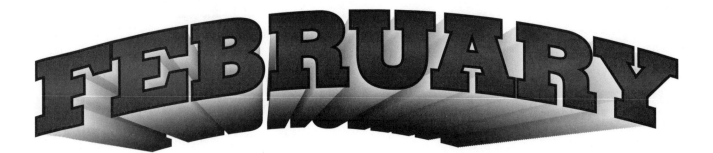

## FEBRUARY

## a creative idea book
## for the
## elementary teacher

written and illustrated
by
**Karen Sevaly**

edited by
**Shelley Price**

Copyright © 1988, 1997
Teacher's Friend Publications, Inc.
All rights reserved.
Printed in the United States of America
Published by Teacher's Friend Publications, Inc.
3240 Trade Center Dr., Riverside, CA 92507

**ISBN-0-943263-05-0**

This book is dedicated
to teachers and children
everywhere.

# Table of Contents

# Making the most of it!

## WHAT IS IN THIS BOOK:

You will find the following in each monthly idea book from Teacher's Friend Publications:

1. A calendar listing every day of the month with a classroom idea and mention of special holidays and events.

2. At least four student awards to be sent home to parents.

3. Three or more bookmarks that can be used in your school library or given to students by you as "Super Student Awards."

4. Numerous bulletin board ideas and patterns pertaining to the particular month and seasonal activity.

5. Easy-to-make craft ideas related to the monthly holidays and special days.

6. Dozens of activities emphasizing not only the obvious holidays but also the often forgotten celebrations such as Ground Hog Day and Dental Health Month.

7. Creative writing pages, crossword puzzles, word finds, booklet covers, games, paper bag puppets, literature lists and much more!

8. Scores of classroom management techniques and methods proven to motivate your students to improve behavior and classroom work.

## HOW TO USE THIS BOOK:

Every page of this book may be duplicated for individual classroom use.

Some pages are meant to be copied or used as duplicating masters. Other pages may be transferred onto construction paper or used as they are.

If you have access to a print shop, you will find that many pages work well when printed on index paper. This type of paper takes crayons and felt markers well and is sturdy enough to last. (Bookmarks work particularly well on index paper.)

Lastly, some pages are meant to be enlarged with an overhead or opaque projector. When we say enlarge, we mean it! Think BIG! Three, four or even five feet is great! Try using colored butcher paper or poster board so you don't spend all your time coloring.

## MONTHLY ORGANIZERS:

Staying organized month after month, year after year can be a real challenge. Try this simple idea:

After using the loose pages from this book, file them in their own file folder labeled with the month's name. This will also provide a place to save pages from other reproducible books along with craft ideas, recipes and articles you find in magazines and periodicals. (*Essential Pocket Folders* by Teacher's Friend provide a perfect way to store your monthly ideas and reproducibles. Each *Monthly Essential Pocket Folder* comes with a sixteen-page booklet of essential patterns and organizational ideas. There are even special folders for *Back to School*, *The Substitute Teacher* and *Parent-Teacher Conferences*.)

You might also like to dedicate a file box for every month of the school year. A covered box will provide room to store large patterns, sample art projects, certificates and awards, monthly stickers, monthly idea books and much more.

## BULLETIN BOARDS IDEAS:

Creating clever bulletin boards for your classroom need not take fantastic amounts of time and money. With a little preparation and know-how, you can have different boards each month with very little effort. Try some of these ideas:

1. Background paper should be put up only once a year. Choose colors that can go with many themes and holidays. The black butcher paper background you used as a spooky display in October will have a special dramatic effect in April with student-made, paper-cut butterflies.

2. Butcher paper is not the only thing that can be used to cover the back of your board. You might also try fabric from a colorful bed sheet or gingham material. Just fold it up at the end of the year to reuse again. Wallpaper is another great background cover. Discontinued rolls can be purchased for a small amount at discount hardware stores. Most can be wiped clean and will not fade like construction paper. (Do not glue wallpaper directly to the board; just staple or pin in place.)

3. Store your bulletin board pieces in large, flat envelopes made from two large sheets of tagboard or cardboard. Simply staple three sides together and slip the pieces inside. (Small pieces can be stored in zip-lock, plastic bags.) Label your large envelopes with the name of the bulletin board and the month and year you displayed it. Take a picture of each bulletin board display. Staple the picture to your storage envelope. Next year when you want to create the same display, you will know right where everything goes. Kids can even follow your directions when you give them a picture to look at.

## ADDING THE COLOR:

Putting the color to finished items can be a real bother to teachers in a rush. Try these ideas:

1. On small areas, watercolor markers work great. If your area is rather large, switch to crayons or even colored chalk or pastels.

   (Don't worry, lamination or a spray fixative will keep color on the work and off of you. No laminator or fixative? That's okay, a little hair spray will do the trick.)

2. The quickest method of coloring large items is to start with colored paper. (Poster board, butcher paper or large construction paper work well.) Add a few dashes of a contrasting colored marker or crayon and you will have it made.

3. Try cutting character eyes, teeth, etc. from white typing paper and gluing them in place. These features will really stand out and make your bulletin boards come alive.

   For special effects, add real buttons or lace. Metallic paper looks great on stars and belt buckles, too.

## LAMINATION:

If you have access to a roll laminator, then you already know how fortunate you are. They are priceless when it comes to saving time and money. Try these ideas:

1. You can laminate more than just classroom posters and construction paper. Try various kinds of fabric, wallpaper and gift wrapping. You'll be surprised at the great combinations you come up with.

   Laminated classified ads can be used to cut headings for current events bulletin boards. Colorful gingham fabric makes terrific cut letters or bulletin board trim. You might even try burlap! Bright foil gift wrapping paper will add a festive feeling to any bulletin board.

   (You can even make professional looking bookmarks with laminated fabric or burlap. They are great holiday gift ideas for Mom or Dad!)

2. Felt markers and laminated paper or fabric can work as a team. Just make sure the markers you use are permanent and not water-based. Oops, make a mistake! That's okay. Put a little ditto fluid on a tissue, rub across the mark and presto, it's gone! Also, dry transfer markers work great on lamination and can easily be wiped off.

## LAMINATION:
## (continued)

3. Laminating cut-out characters can be tricky. If you have enlarged an illustration onto poster board, simply laminate first and then cut it out with scissors or an art knife. (Just make sure the laminator is hot enough to create a good seal.)

One problem may arise when you paste an illustration onto poster board and laminate the finished product. If your paste-up is not 100% complete, your illustration and posterboard may separate after laminating. To avoid this problem, paste your illustration onto poster board that measures slightly larger than the illustration. This way, the lamination will help hold down your paste-up.

4. When pasting up your illustration, always try to use either rubber cement, artist's spray adhesive or a glue stick. White glue, tape or paste does not laminate well because it can often be seen under your artwork.

5. Have you ever laminated student-made place mats, crayon shavings, tissue paper collages, or dried flowers? You'll be amazed at the variety of creative things that can be laminated and used in the classroom or as take-home gifts.

## PHOTOCOPIES AND
## DITTO MASTERS:

Many of the pages in this book can be copied for use in the classroom. Try some of these ideas for best results:

1. If the print from the back side of your original comes through the front when making a photocopy or ditto master, slip a sheet of black construction paper behind the sheet. This will mask the unwanted shadows and create a much better copy.

2. Several potential masters in this book contain instructions for the teacher. Simply cover the type with correction fluid or a small slip of paper before duplicating.

3. When using a new ditto master, turn down the pressure on the duplicating machine. As the copies become light, increase the pressure. This will get longer wear out of both the master and the machine.

4. Trying to squeeze one more run out of that worn ditto master can be frustrating. Try lightly spraying the inked side of the master with hair spray. For some reason, this helps the master put out those few extra copies.

## LETTERING AND HEADINGS:

Not every school has a letter machine that produces perfect 4" letters. The rest of us will just have to use the old stencil-and-scissor method. But wait, there is an easier way!

1. Don't cut individual letters as they are difficult to pin up straight, anyway. Instead, hand print bulletin board titles and headings onto strips of colored paper. When it is time for the board to come down, simply roll it up to use again next year. If you buy your own pre-cut lettering, save yourself some time and hassle by pasting the desired statements onto long strips of colored paper. Laminate if possible. These can be rolled up and stored the same way!

   Use your imagination! Try cloud shapes and cartoon bubbles. They will all look great.

2. Hand lettering is not that difficult, even if your printing is not up to penmanship standards. Print block letters with a felt marker. Draw big dots at the end of each letter. This will hide any mistakes and add a charming touch to the overall effect.

   If you are still afraid to freehand it, try this nifty idea: Cut a strip of poster board about 28" X 6". Down the center of the strip, cut a window with an art knife measuring 20" X 2". There you have it: a perfect stencil for any lettering job. All you need to do is write capital letters with a felt marker within the window slot. Don't worry about uniformity. Just fill up the entire window height with your letters. Move your poster-board strip along as you go. The letters will always remain straight and even because the poster board window is straight.

3. If you must cut individual letters, use construction paper squares measuring 4 1/2" X 6". (Laminate first if you can.) Cut the capital letters as shown. No need to measure; irregular letters will look creative and not messy.

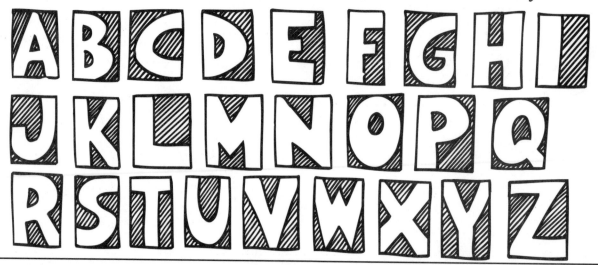

# Calendar

# FEBRUARY

**1ST**  LANGSTON HUGHES, famous American black poet, was born on this day in 1902. (Find one of his poems in the school library and read it to your class.)

**2ND**  Today is GROUNDHOG DAY! (Tell your class the legend of the groundhog and its shadow. Ask students to bring in newspaper articles about the event.)

**3RD**  Famous American artist NORMAN ROCKWELL was born on this day in 1894. (Find a print of one of Mr. Rockwell's well-known paintings and have your students write a creative story about it.)

**4TH**  CHARLES LINDBERGH, the first person to make a solo non-stop flight across the Atlantic Ocean, was born on this day in 1902. (Ask your students to find out the name of Mr. Lindbergh's plane.)

**5TH**  "Home Run King" HANK AARON was born on this day in 1934. (Ask baseball fans to find out how many home runs he hit during his career.)

**6TH**  Today marks the birthdate of American President RONALD REAGAN in 1911. (Ask students to find out how old he is today.)

**7TH**  LAURA INGALLS WILDER, author of the "*Little House*" books, was born on this day in 1867. (Suggest these wonderful books to your students on your next library visit.)

**8TH**  The BOY SCOUTS OF AMERICA were incorporated on this day in 1910. (Ask someone from the local Boy Scout office to visit your class and tell about the many programs offered for both boys and girls.)

**9TH**  The United States government established the NATIONAL WEATHER SERVICE on this day in 1870. (Ask a group of students to research how weather forecasting has changed in the last one-hundred years.)

**10TH**  The first SINGING TELEGRAM was delivered in New York City on this day in 1933. (Ask students to write a funny singing telegram to the tune of a familiar song and sing it to the class.)

**11**<sup>TH</sup> THOMAS ALVA EDISON, American inventor, was born on this day in 1847. (Have students research at least ten of his more than 1,100 inventions!)

**12**<sup>TH</sup> ABRAHAM LINCOLN, 16th president of the United States, was born on this day in 1809. (Have students make "Penny Medallions" in celebration of this great man's birthday.)

**13**<sup>TH</sup> "THE AMERICAN MAGAZINE," the first magazine in the United States, was published on this day in 1741. (Set up a magazine corner in your classroom that will appeal to a variety of interests.)

**14**<sup>TH</sup> Today is ST. VALENTINE'S DAY! (Give someone a very special valentine by doing something especially nice for him or her.)

**15**<sup>TH</sup> Today marks the birthdate of SUSAN B. ANTHONY, early women's rights leader, in 1820. (Pass a Susan B. Anthony dollar around the class as you tell about this heroic woman.)

**16**<sup>TH</sup> The first television news program was broadcast on this day in 1948. (Ask several students to role-play being "television newscasters." Have them research current events and report their findings to the class.)

**17**<sup>TH</sup> The Parent Teacher Association, P.T.A., was established on this day in 1897. (Your students might like to write a note to your school's PTA board, thanking them for all their good work.)

**18**<sup>TH</sup> The planet PLUTO was seen for the first time by astronomer Clyde Tombaugh in 1930. (Ask students to find out how far Pluto is from the sun.)

**19**<sup>TH</sup> Polish astronomer NICHOLAUS COPERNICUS was born on this day in 1473. (Ask students to find out what he discovered about our solar system.)

**20**<sup>TH</sup> United States astronaut JOHN GLENN became the first person to orbit the earth on this day in 1962. (Ask students to find out the name of his spacecraft.)

**21**<sup>ST</sup> Today marks the birthdate of CESAR CHAVEZ, noted Mexican-American social activist who led the organization of the National Farm Workers Union. (Older students may wish to participate in a discussion about unions in the United States.)

**22**<sup>ND</sup> GEORGE WASHINGTON, the first president of the United States was born on this day in 1732. (Have each child make a three-cornered hat to wear in celebration.)

**23<sup>RD</sup>**  German-English composer GEORGE FREDERICK HANDEL was born on this day in 1685. (Find a recording of one of his great compositions and play it during silent reading time.)

**24<sup>TH</sup>**  Today is MEXICAN FLAG DAY! (Find a picture of the Mexican flag to display in your classroom today!)

**25<sup>TH</sup>**  The RANGER, the first United States aircraft carrier, was launched on this day in 1934. (Ask students to find out how large most aircraft carriers are and compare them to the size of your school's playground.)

**26<sup>TH</sup>**  Congress designated the GRAND CANYON as a National Park on this day in 1919. (Ask students to locate the Grand Canyon on the classroom map.)

**27<sup>TH</sup>**  Today marks the birthdate of HENRY WADSWORTH LONGFELLOW, author of "The Song of Hiawatha" and "Paul Revere's Ride." (Read one of these famous works to your class.)

**28<sup>TH</sup>**  The first gold-seekers arrived in San Francisco, California, marking the beginning of the GOLDRUSH in 1849. (Ask a student to locate San Francisco on the classroom map.)

**29<sup>TH</sup>**  Today is "LEAP YEAR," which occurs only every four years. (Ask students if they would like to have been born on February 29th.)

Mardi Gras (Fat Tuesday) - Begins on Shrove Tuesday, the day before Lent, a forty day period of abstinence before Easter Sunday.

FEBRUARY IS ALSO.....

AFRICAN-AMERICAN MONTH

NATIONAL HEART MONTH

CHILDREN'S DENTAL HEALTH MONTH

NATIONAL PATRIOTISM WEEK (Third Week of February)

BROTHERHOOD-SISTERHOOD WEEK (Third Week of February)

INTERNATIONAL FRIENDSHIP WEEK (Fourth Week of February)

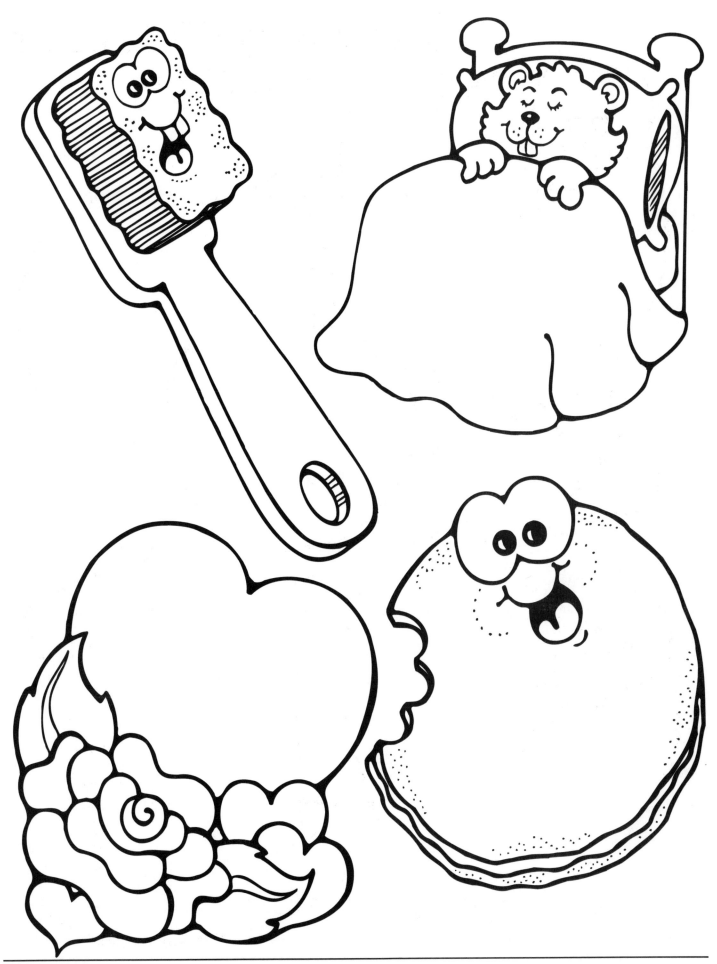

# February

| Sunday | Monday | Tuesday | Wednesday | Thursday | Friday | Saturday |
|--------|--------|---------|-----------|----------|--------|----------|
|        |        |         |           |          |        |          |
|        |        |         |           |          |        |          |
|        |        |         |           |          |        |          |
|        |        |         |           |          |        |          |
|        |        |         |           |          |        |          |

# February Activities!

February Fun!

# February Activities!

The month of February offers a wide variety of special days and celebrations. The holidays of Ground Hog Day, Presidents' Day and Valentine's Day can all be used to motivate creativity and reinforce basic concepts in the classroom. This is a good thing, considering that February often has the worst weather of the year! So take advantage of the many special days in February and prepare for a colorful month of fun activities!

## February Crossword

## DOWN
1. What you give on February 14th.
2. The 16th President of the U.S.
3. He looks for his shadow on February 2nd.
4. A muscle that pumps blood.

## ACROSS
1. The "Father of Our Country."
2. The weather in February is usually _____.
3. Baby birds live in a _____.
4. What you brush every morning.
5. The opposite of "hate."
6. The doctor that checks your teeth.

# February Word Find!

FIND THESE FEBRUARY WORDS IN THE PUZZLE BELOW:
VALENTINE, FEBRUARY, WASHINGTON, LINCOLN, GROUNDHOG,
HEART, CUPID, SHADOW, LOVE, CHERRY, WINTER AND SNOW.

```
A Z X C D F V W A S H I N G T O N V D F T G
A X V S E R F B N M J K L O P T Y G H B W E
C D A R F G H J K C U P I D C V B N H Y I G
W C L T Y U I V D F G H Y R V B N M F S N Y
X V E V B L O V E G Y H R T Y U I K L H T J
C G N Y J K I U F R T E W Q X C V B H J E Y
A F T F B H G Y T N D A G K C X V H Y F R B
F T I F B H N J N M U R F G H J K L O D T U
G J N V G T Y H J U Y T C F D E S R T H Y U
S C E G G R O U N D H O G V H Y T E W Q C V
C B H Y U J M L S V B H Y U I O P L K J M G
S D C H E R R Y N J I K F D S W Q A C B G D
X V F T G B N M O U Y T R E W Q F G H J K L
A S H A D O W R W F G H B N M K J I U K L O
B N H J K L O I U J K M N B G L I N C O L N
S C V G Y H N M J K I U Y T G F R E D C V B
S C V G F E B R U A R Y G B N J U G R E W D
```

# February Bingo!

This game offers a fun way to cheer up a gloomy day in February. Give each child a copy of the bingo words listed below or write the words on the chalkboard. Ask students to write any 24 words on his or her bingo card. Use the same directions you might use for regular bingo.

## FEBRUARY BINGO WORDS

| | | | |
|---|---|---|---|
| VALENTINE | WASHINGTON | LINCOLN | GROUND HOG |
| HEART | GEORGE | ABRAHAM | SHADOW |
| FEBRUARY | CHERRY TREE | LOG CABIN | AFRAID |
| CUPID | PRESIDENT | ILLINOIS | WINTER |
| LOVE | MARTHA | MARY TODD | SPRING |
| CANDY | GENERAL | HONEST | LEAP YEAR |
| FLOWERS | HERO | CIVIL WAR | MONTH |
| LACE | INDEPENDENCE | FREEDOM | SHORT |

# FEBRUARY
# BINGO

FREE

# Pencil Toppers

Reproduce these "Pencil Toppers" onto construction or index paper. Color and cut out. Use an art knife to cut through the Xs.

Slide a pencil through both Xs, as shown.

Give them as classroom awards or birthday treats.

WAKE UP! VISIT THE LIBRARY!

Mr. Groundhog

Zzzzz

I'm a Book Lover!

---

Student's Name

was a "sweetheart" in class today!

Date

Teacher

---

Student's Name

earned my praise today!

For: _____

_____

Date

Teacher

---

Student's Name

was extra good today!

Teacher

Date

---

I was all smiles because... _____

_____

_____

Teacher          Date

---

# STUDENT
## OF THE
# MONTH

NAME

SCHOOL

DATE

TEACHER

# CERTIFICATE

## OF AWARD

### presented to

NAME

### in recognition of

TEACHER

DATE

# CITIZENSHIP AWARD

NAME

has demonstrated good citizenship by

TEACHER

DATE

# February Paper Topper

Here's a cute way to display students' work!

Cut these Paper Toppers from colored paper or students can use crayons or markers to add the color.

Fold along the dotted lines, tape the back together and insert over the corner of a student's good work paper! Display the papers with the topper on the class board.

# Creative Writing Page

# Groundhog Day!

# Groundhog Day - February 2nd!

The legend of the groundhog has been traced back many years to the folk stories of England and Germany. It was believed that hibernating animals would wake on this day, check the weather and then decide whether to go back to sleep for the rest of the winter or stay up for the coming of spring.

According to the legend, if the weather is cloudy and the groundhog cannot see its shadow, it will stay above ground. This signifies the early coming of spring. If it's sunny outside and the groundhog sees its shadow, it will be startled and quickly retreat to its burrow below ground, staying there six more weeks. This means that spring is a long way away and at least six more weeks of winter will remain.

The custom of groundhog watching on February 2nd was brought to the United States by immigrants. These immigrants settled in Punxsutawney Pennsylvania. In recent years, the town of Punxsutawney has been crowded with tourists and news reporters waiting the news of whether or not Punxsutawney Phil (the world's most famous groundhog) will see his shadow.

If you wish to find out more about the Groundhog Day tradition and Punxsutawney Phil, write to his fan club. You can also subscribe to his fan club newsletter.

Your students can also investigate Punxsutawney Phil's web site at http//www.groundhog.org

Phil's Fan Club
Punxsutawney Groundhog Club
Chamber of Commerce
124 W. Mahoning Street
Punxsutawney, PA 15767

On February 2nd, ask your students to record the weather. Would the famous groundhog be able to see his shadow? Take a vote and record the results on the class board noting the students' guess of whether spring will come early or if there will be six more weeks of winter. Now, assign students to record the weather for the next six weeks. How did your students fare? Was Punxsutawney Phil prediction correct?

# Groundhog Paper Bag Puppet

# Groundhog Pattern

My Groundhog Day Prediction

_____

_____

_____

_____

_____

_____

Name

# Groundhog Activities!

## GROUNDHOG DAY BULLETIN BOARD

Create a cute and informative bulletin board using the groundhog pattern on the previous page.

Cover the class bulletin board with green butcher paper. Carefully cut slits in the paper using an art knife. After the students

have completed writing their predictions on the groundhog patterns, have them insert their groundhogs into the slits on the board. Students can add grass and flowers using colored chalk or crayons. Post a class weather chart on the board and record each day's weather for six weeks after Groundhog Day. At the end of the six weeks, determine whether spring came early or late. Lift the groundhog characters from their holes to see which students predicted correctly.

## GROUNDHOG POP-UP CRAFT

Students will love making this adorable groundhog puppet!

Glue a fringed strip of greeN construction paper to the outside of a small styrofoam drinking cup. Cut the groundhog from brown paper and glue it to an ice cream stick. Place the stick through the slit in the bottom of the cup.

Children will love to hold the cup and slide the stick up and down to make the groundhog come out of its hole.

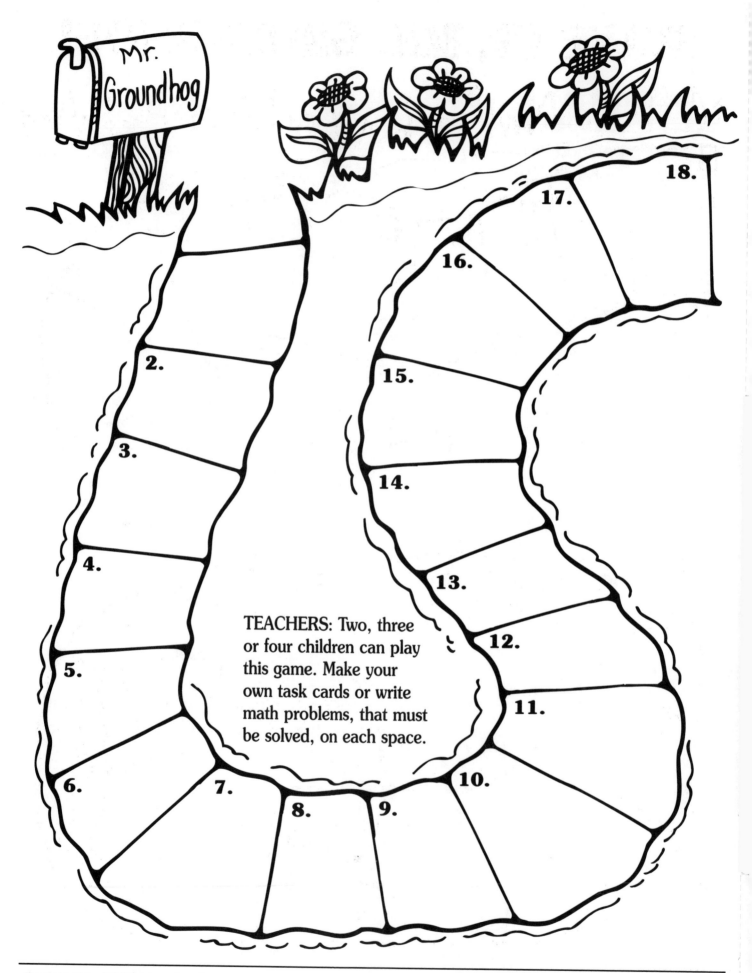

**Mr. Groundhog**

2.

3.

4.

5.

6.

7.

8.

9.

10.

11.

12.

13.

14.

15.

16.

17.

18.

TEACHERS: Two, three or four children can play this game. Make your own task cards or write math problems, that must be solved, on each space.

# WAKE UP, MR. GROUNDHOG!

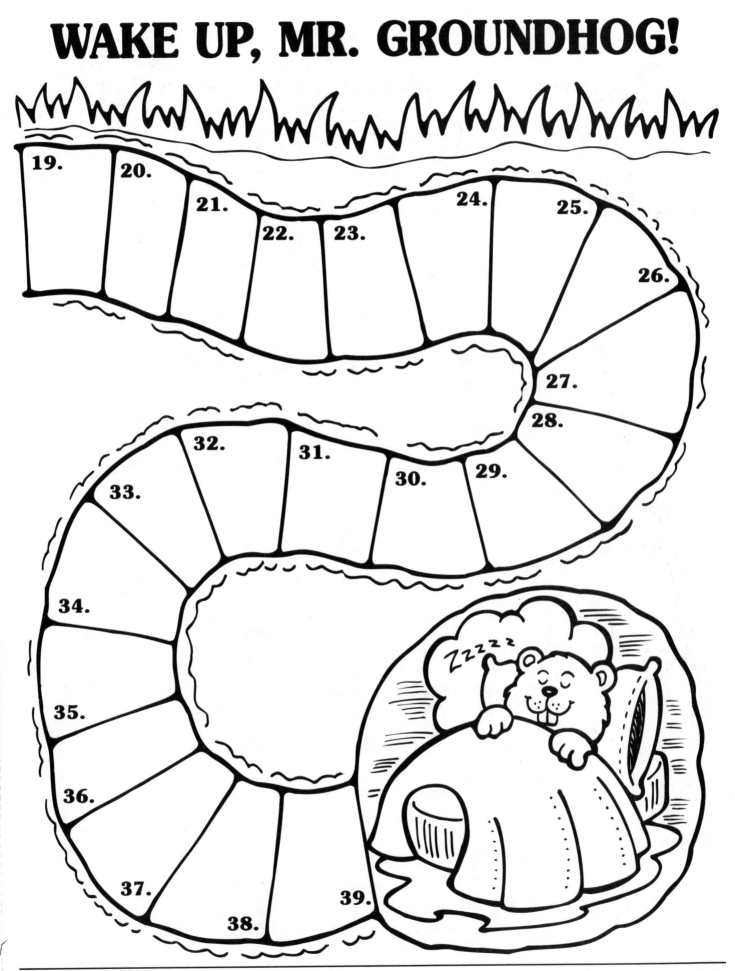

# Groundhog Maze

40

# Me and My SHADOW!

I am _____ feet and _____ inches tall.

A friend helped me measure my shadow at different times during the day. This is what I found out.

| Time | Length of my shadow |
|------|---------------------|
|      |                     |
|      |                     |
|      |                     |
|      |                     |
|      |                     |
|      |                     |

My shadow was longest at _____.

My shadow was shortest at _____.

Here is a poem about my shadow.:

_____

_____

_____

_____

_____

# My Weather Record

| Date | Sunny | Cloudy | Rainy | Snowy | Windy | Temperature High | Temperature Low |
|------|-------|--------|-------|-------|-------|------|-----|
|      |       |        |       |       |       |      |     |
|      |       |        |       |       |       |      |     |
|      |       |        |       |       |       |      |     |
|      |       |        |       |       |       |      |     |
|      |       |        |       |       |       |      |     |
|      |       |        |       |       |       |      |     |
|      |       |        |       |       |       |      |     |
|      |       |        |       |       |       |      |     |
|      |       |        |       |       |       |      |     |
|      |       |        |       |       |       |      |     |
|      |       |        |       |       |       |      |     |
|      |       |        |       |       |       |      |     |

Name

# Abraham Lincoln!

# Abraham Lincoln - February 12, 1809!

Abraham Lincoln is thought by most Americans to be one of our greatest presidents. He was born on February 12, 1809, in a rural area now known as the state of Kentucky. Lincoln had a special love for reading and spent many evenings by the fire with his favorite books. He taught himself many things, including law, using the books he read. As a young man, Lincoln split rails and worked as a clerk in a general store. His kind nature and honesty gained him the respect of local townspeople.

In 1834, Lincoln was elected to the House of Representatives and later senator from the state of Illinois. In 1860, Americans voted in Abraham Lincolnas our 16th president.

Lincoln was an impressive man, standing six feet and four inches. He had a high-pitched voice and deep-set eyes. When he stood to speak, people were astonished by his grand appearance.

Abraham Lincoln was a man of great insight, intelligence and wit. He was able, quite easily, to bring his ideas to the people through his speeches. One of his best known speeches is the Gettysburg Address. He was most famous for the Emancipation Proclamation which helped free slaves after the Abraham Lincoln was shot by an assassin on April 14, 1865. It is unfortunate (in) that he did not live to see the fulfillment of his dream: the abolition of slavery. War.

## LINCOLN PENNY MEDALLIONS

Have each child cut this pattern from red or blue construction paper. Give each child a new penny and ask them to glue it, Lincoln side up, to the center. Punch a hole at the top of each medallion and thread with yarn.

Children will love wearing these easy to make medallions to celebrate Lincoln's birthday.

# Abe's Whiskers!

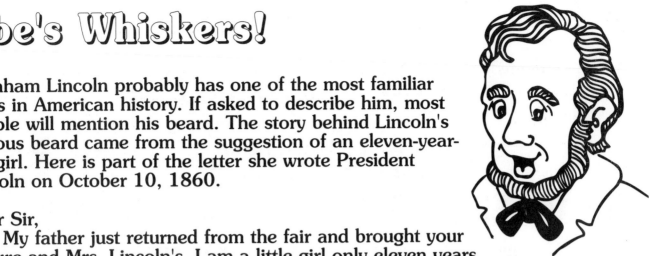

Abraham Lincoln probably has one of the most familiar faces in American history. If asked to describe him, most people will mention his beard. The story behind Lincoln's famous beard came from the suggestion of an eleven-year-old girl. Here is part of the letter she wrote President Lincoln on October 10, 1860.

Dear Sir,
      My father just returned from the fair and brought your picture and Mrs. Lincoln's. I am a little girl only eleven years old but want you to be president very much--so I hope you won't think me very bold to write to such a great man as you are. I have four brothers and part of them will vote for you any way--and if you let your whiskers grow I will try and get the rest of them to vote for you. And you would look a great deal better for your face is so thin...
      I must not write any more. Answer this letter right off. Good-bye.
                            Grace Bedell

President Lincoln responded to Grace's request. She received the following letter a few days later:

My Dear Little Miss,
      Your very agreeable letter...is received. I regret the necessity of saying I have no daughters. I have three sons. They, with their mother, constitute my whole family.
      As to the whiskers, having never worn any, do you not think people would call it a piece of silly affectation if I were to begin it now?
                            Your very sincere well wisher,
                            A. Lincoln

Grace may have been a little disappointed in her letter from Lincoln, but she was delighted when he visited her in person a few months later. To her surprise, Mr. Lincoln had grown whiskers just as she had suggested.

It could be said that Grace Bedell was a young girl that changed the face of American history!

---

Have your students discuss the correspondence of Grace Bedell and President Lincoln. What other questions could Grace have asked the President?

Encourage your pupils to write to the current President of the United States, one of their state's senators or their local member of the House of Representatives. They may wish to ask about his or her stand on a certain issue or simply wish them well. Mail the letters to The President of the United States, 1600 Pennsylvania Blvd. N.W., Washington D.C. 20500 or find the local congressperson's address in your neighborhood newspaper.

# The Gettysburg Address!

# Abraham Lincoln, November 19, 1863
# Gettysburg, Pennsylvania

Four score and seven years ago our fathers brought forth on this continent a new nation, conceived in Liberty, and dedicated to the proposition that all men are created equal.

Now we are engaged in a great civil war, testing whether that nation or any nation so conceived and so dedicated, can long endure. We are met on a great battle-field of that war. We have come to dedicate a portion of that field, as a final resting place for those who here gave their lives that that nation might live. It is altogether fitting and proper that we should do this.

But, in a larger sense, we can not dedicate--we can not consecrate--we can not hallow--this ground. The brave men, living and dead, who struggled here, have consecrated it, far above our poor power to add or detract. The world will little note, nor long remember what we say here, but it can never forget what they did here. It is for us the living, rather, to be dedicated here to the unfinished work which they who fought here have thus far so nobly advanced. It is rather for us to be here dedicated to the great task remaining before us--that from these honored dead we take increased devotion to that cause for which they gave the last full measure of devotion--that we highly resolve that these dead shall not have died in vain--that this nation, under God, shall have a new birth of freedom--and that government of the people, by the people, for the people, shall not perish from the earth.

Abraham Lincoln

FOLD

Name

# Lincoln's Beard and Hat

Make a top hat from black construction paper measuring 22" x 8" and tape to form a cylinder. Cut a large circle from paper about 14" in diameter. Cut a smaller circle inside. Cut the notches around the inner circle and fold upward to fit inside the cylinder. Use tape to hold in place.

Children will love dressing up like Lincoln, especially on February 12th.

Cut this beard pattern from black construction paper. Curl the ends around your ears to hold in place.

## LINCOLN PENNIES

Everyone has seen Lincoln's face on shiny new pennies. Cut several large circles from light-brown construction paper. Use this pattern to trace Lincoln's profile in the center of each circle. Display the pennies on the class bulletin board.

## LINCOLN SILHOUETTE

Cut Lincoln's silhouette from colored construction paper. Now, cut the silhouette into several puzzle pieces. Put the pieces in an envelope. As students complete their class work, give them the puzzle to reassemble at their desks.

## LOG CABINS

Make clever Lincoln Log Cabins with small milk cartons and an ample supply of stick pretzels. Ask each child to glue the pretzels to the four sides of their milk carton. Have them break the pretzels the proper length to fit the sides. Add bright red construction paper roofs to the finished cabins.

## READING LIKE LINCOLN

As a child and young man, Lincoln loved to sit by the fire and read various stories and books. Some of his favorite stories were from *Aesop's Fables*. Read one or two of these fables to your class and discuss how these stories may have inspired Lincoln in the way he viewed his fellow man and life in general.

## FAMOUS QUOTES

Lincoln was famous for his wit and insight. Write several of his quotations on the class chalkboard and ask students to write their feelings about what Lincoln meant and perhaps what significance it might have for the world today.

Here are a few of Lincoln's quotes:

"No man has a good enough memory to be a successful liar."

"Better to remain silent and be thought a fool than to speak out and remove all doubt."

"Killing the dog does not cure the bite."

"As I would not be a slave, so I would not be a master."

"It is true that you may fool all the people some of the time; you can even fool some of the people all of the time; but you can't fool all of the people all of the time."

"Those who deny freedom to others deserve it not for themselves."

# Lincoln Activities

# Abraham Lincoln

## Activity Cards

Teachers: Discuss with your students the history and facts about both George Washington and Abraham Lincoln. Provide these cards for an informative center activity about the two presidents.

Cut out each activity card and mount on colored posterboard. Ask individual students to take the cards to their desks and match the fact cards to the appropriate president card. Two students might like to time one another to see who can match all the cards correctly in the least amount of time.

(Washington cards can be found on pages 60 and 61.)

Washington or Lincoln?

This president was born near Hodgenville, Kentucky on February 12, 1809.

Washington or Lincoln?

This president moved with his family to the state of Illinois in 1831.

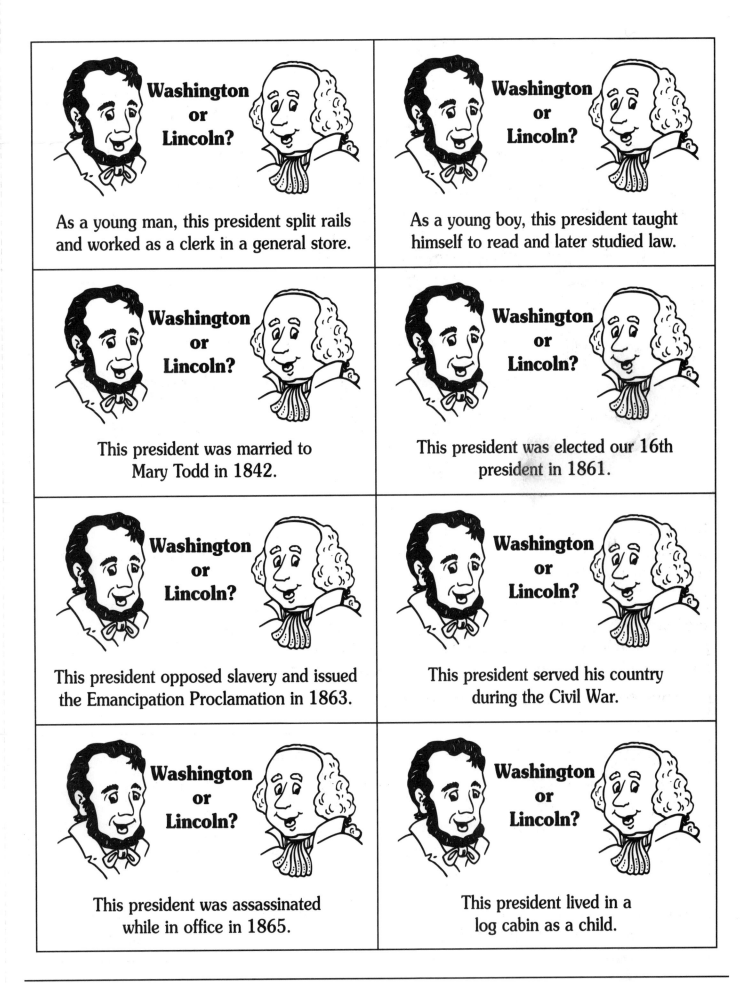

**Washington or Lincoln?**

As a young man, this president split rails and worked as a clerk in a general store.

**Washington or Lincoln?**

As a young boy, this president taught himself to read and later studied law.

**Washington or Lincoln?**

This president was married to Mary Todd in 1842.

**Washington or Lincoln?**

This president was elected our 16th president in 1861.

**Washington or Lincoln?**

This president opposed slavery and issued the Emancipation Proclamation in 1863.

**Washington or Lincoln?**

This president served his country during the Civil War.

**Washington or Lincoln?**

This president was assassinated while in office in 1865.

**Washington or Lincoln?**

This president lived in a log cabin as a child.

# Lincoln's Cabin

Cut "Lincoln's Cabin" out and assemble it on a sheet of construction paper. Cut the window out and fold back along the dotted lines. Glue a shiny new "Lincoln" penny to the center of the window. Students may like to glue stick pretzels to the cabin to make it resemble a real "log cabin.

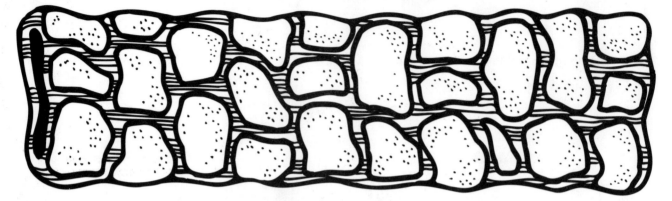

Display dozens of log cabins on the class bulletin board to create an entire village!

Paste the chimney to the side of the cabin.

# "Abe"

HONEST ABE!

Display "Abe" on the class bulletin board or have each student make their own "Abe" character.

# My Report About Lincoln

_____
Student's Name

**Abraham Lincoln was born on**

_____
Date

**in a rural area now known as the**

**state of** _____.

**As a young man, he loved to**

_____ **by firelight. He taught himself many things**

**including** _____.

**He was elected to the** _____  _____

**in 1834 and later Senator from** _____.

**Lincoln was elected** _____ **in** _____ **and**

**became the 16th President of the United States.**

**His most famous speech was the** _____

_____ . **His most famous accomplishment**

**was the** _____ **Proclamation. This**

**Proclamation helped** _____.

**Just a few day after the end of the** _____ **War,**

**President Lincoln was** _____.

**My thoughts about President Lincoln:** _____

_____

_____

_____

# George Washington!

# George Washington - February 22, 1732!

George Washington is known throughout American history as "The Father of Our Country." He was born on February 22, 1732 in Westmoreland County, Virginia. As a young man, Washington had a great interest in military history and geography. He became a surveyor at the age of seventeen. Washington played an important role during the French and Indian War. This experience later gave him the knowledge and insight to assist the fight for freedom during the American Revolution. Washington served as Commander in Chief of the Continental Armies. America won its independence from England with the signing of the Declaration of Independence in 1776.

*He also married a woman named Martha*

George Washington was elected and served as the first president of the United States. His birthday was celebrated throughout our young country, even during his own lifetime. Today, we pay tribute to this great man on the third Monday in February.

The story of George Washington and his greatness is known throughout the world. The capital of the United States is honored with his name. In Washington, D.C., an inspiring monument stands, the symbol of reverence and affection for our first president. Washington is remembered in the hearts of all Americans as a man of honesty, strength and leadership. *+ as the father of our country.*

Like George Washington... I cannot tell a lie!

Name

**"I CANNOT TELL A LIE!"**
Tell your class the story of George Washington and his father's cherry tree. Stress the importance of George's refusal to tell a lie about what he had done.

Each child will enjoy wearing the "I cannot tell a lie!" button after taking a pledge to always tell the truth. This is a wonderful way to celebrate Washington's birthday.

# Washington Word Find!

```
D F G V B N M H J K L M N B V L E A D E R
W S D F G H N J K F G H B N M K L O P U G
A D F R E T G H F A T H E R D R F G Y H E
S U R V E Y O R E V G B H N J U T R F B O
H S D Q W E S F B D V R T Y H N M J K L R
I F G H Y T D F R F G B H N J N M K J C G
N X F D G E D B U X C F R E E D O M F O E
G C F V C V N N A R Y D V F G B H N J U K
T Y H N B G F D R S X C V F G B H Y T N Q
O V H R G I W I Y F R G T H B N M J K T I
N P R E S I D E N T V G T H Y U J K I R L
X C V B N M J H G F V I R G I N I A E Y T
A X C D F V B G H N M J K L P O I Y T R E
S W D F V G B I N D E P E N D E N C E T Y
S V B H G S X C R E D V B H G T R G H B N
D E C L A R A T I O N D F V C S A X E T F
A C D S E T G B A M E R I C A F R E D S E
```

## ACTIVITY 4

FIND THESE WORDS ABOUT WASHINGTON: GEORGE, WASHINGTON, FEBRUARY, VIRGINIA, FREEDOM, INDEPENDENCE, DECLARATION, SURVEYOR, PRESIDENT, COUNTRY, LEADER, FATHER, AMERICA

Lincoln
and
Washington
Finger
Puppets!

Cut Out  Cut Out

Cut Out  Cut Out

## PRESIDENT'S DAY

Until recently, Washington's birthday was observed on February 22 and Lincoln's birthday on February 12. In 1971, these holidays were replaced by President's Day, the third Monday in February. Ask students to discuss their opinions of this change. What benefits might there be? What disadvantages?

## PATRIOTIC SONGS

Locate a recording of popular patriotic tunes such as "Yankee Doodle," "America the Beautiful," "Battle Hymn of the Republic," "America," and "The Star Spangled Banner." Play these songs for your class and ask them to find out how the songs came to be written.

## WASHINGTON'S SILHOUETTE

Trace Washington's silhouette onto colored construction paper. Fill in the silhouette with small squares of contrasting tissue paper. First place one square around the end of a pencil. Dip into white glue and place on the silhouette. Continue until the entire silhouette is complete. Display on the class bulletin board.

## W-A-S-H-I-N-G-T-O-N

Write the letters W-A-S-H-I-N-G-T-O-N down the side of a sheet of lined paper. Ask children to write a sentence about George Washington, using the letters of his name.

## WASHINGTON VOCABULARY

Ask students to locate vocabulary words about Washington in the class dictionary. Write the words and definitions on strips of colored paper and display them around Washington's silhouette on the class bulletin board. Here are a few words that your students might wish to use:

CONSTITUTION    SURVEYOR    DIPLOMAT

INDEPENDENCE    REVOLUTION

DECLARATION    MONUMENT    STATESMAN

PRESIDENT    DEDICATION    GENERAL

HONESTY    MILITARY    FREEDOM

# Washington Activities

# Three-Cornered Cap

Cut three hat patterns from blue or black construction paper. Staple the corners together to form a three-cornered hat, much like the one worn by George Washington.

Glue a yellow paper star to each corner of the hat for decorations.

# George Washington

## Activity Cards

Teachers: Discuss with your students the history and facts about both George Washington and Abraham Lincoln. Provide these cards for an informative center activity about the two presidents.

Cut out each activity card and mount on colored posterboard. Ask individual students to take the cards to their desks and match the fact cards to the appropriate president card. Two students might like to time one another to see who can match all the cards correctly in the least amount of time.

(Lincoln cards can be found on pages 50 and 51.)

Washington or Lincoln?

This president is known as "The Father of Our Country."

Washington or Lincoln?

This president was born in Virginia, on February 22, 1732.

**Washington or Lincoln?**

This president signed the Declaration of Independence.

**Washington or Lincoln?**

This president was Commander and Chief of the Continental Armies during the Revolutionary War.

**Washington or Lincoln?**

This president lived on a beautiful plantation called Mount Vernon.

**Washington or Lincoln?**

This president spent the winter of 1777 with his troops at Valley Forge.

**Washington or Lincoln?**

This president married Martha Curtis in 1759.

**Washington or Lincoln?**

This president was the first president of the United States.

**Washington or Lincoln?**

As a young boy, this president refused to lie about cutting down his father's cherry tree.

**Washington or Lincoln?**

As a young man, this president studied geography and mathematics. He became a surveyor at the age of 17.

GEORGE WASHINGTON

_____
Name

FOLD

# "George"

Enlarge "George" onto posterboard. Cut out and color. Display him, as illustrated, on the class bulletin board.

Students might like to make a smaller version of "George" of their very own.

# My Report About Washington

_____
Student's Name

**George Washington was born on**

_____
Date

**in the colony of _____ .**

**As a young man he was said to**

**be very honest and that he never**

**told a _____ .**

**He studied _____ and geography and**

**became a _____ . His wife's name**

**was _____ .**

**He was one of the signers of the _____**

**of _____ .**

**He was elected the first _____ of**

**the _____ of America.**

**He is known as "The _____ of Our Country."**

**Washington was a great man.**

**In his honor, these places and things were named after**

**him:   _____**

_____

_____

_____

_____

# St. Valentine's Day

Be Mine!

# St. Valentine's Day - February 14th!

Many legends surround the history of St. Valentine's Day. One of the most fascinating is that of Saint Valentine himself.

In 269 A.D., a young priest named Valentinus was arrested by the Romans for his Christian beliefs. The Roman Emperor, Claudius II, was a harsh leader and imprisoned Valentinus in a dark dungeon.

A jailer named Asterius took pity on the prisoner and provided him with the company of his blind daughter. The daughter and Valentinus soon became close friends. Their friendship helped sustain Valentinus during his time in prison.

After Valentinus had spent a year in the dungeon, Claudius II summoned him to appear before his court. Claudius was so impressed by the priest's character that he promised to grant him his freedom if he would only denounce Christianity. However, Valentinus refused to give up his belief in God. The Emperor was furious at Valentinus and his stubbornness. He ordered Valentinus to be beaten with stones and executed.

In the last days of his life, St. Valentine is said to have healed Asterius' daughter of blindness and was responsible for converting both of them to Christianity, a decision that later brought on their own deaths, as well.

According to legend, St. Valentine wrote a farewell message to Asterius' daughter the evening of his execution. He signed the note, "From Your Valentine." He was put to death on February 14th, 270 A.D., outside the gates of Rome.

As years went by, the phrase "From Your Valentine" became known as a symbol of love, friendship and affection. St. Valentine is remembered by young and old alike for his devotion and giving nature each year on February 14th.

"LOVE IS PATIENT,
LOVE IS KIND...
LOVE BEARS ALL THINGS,
BELIEVES ALL THINGS,
HOPES ALL THINGS,
ENDURES ALL THINGS.
LOVE NEVER FAILS."

I Corinthians 13:4, 7, 8

# Valentine Crossword!

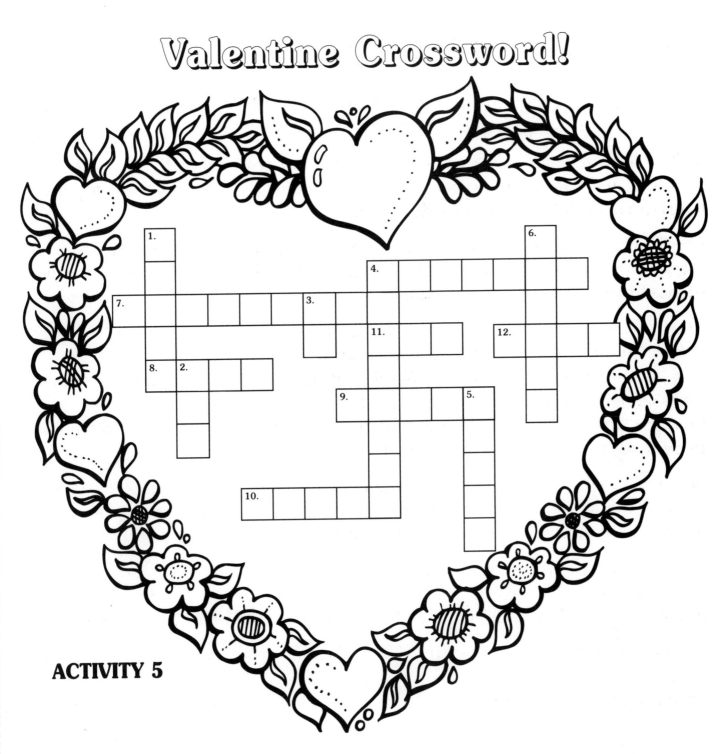

**ACTIVITY 5**

## DOWN
1. We all have a _ _ _ _ _ that beats.
2. Roses are _ _ _ , Violets are blue.
3. The opposite of out.
4. The second month of the year.
5. A flower with many petals.
6. Cupid shoots _ _ _ _ _ _ from a bow.

## ACROSS
4. What blooms in the spring?
7. A sweetheart on February 14th.
8. The opposite of false.
9. The Valentine cherub.
10. Something sweet to eat.
11. Cupid carries a _ _ _ .
12. "I _ _ _ _ You!"

# Valentine Activities!

## VALENTINE SACHET

Boys and girls alike love to sew. Give each child two hearts cut from red or pink felt. Ask them to place the hearts together and stitch the sides with needle and thread. Have them leave a small opening to enclose a cotton ball scented with cologne or some potpourri. They can now stitch up the opening and give it to Mom on Valentine's Day.

## CLASSMATE VALENTINES

Write each students' name on a slip of paper and have each child draw a name. Ask them to write a four-line poem about the person they have chosen, saying only nice things and remaining careful not to mention them by name. When the verses are complete, have each child copy the poem onto a large paper heart and display it on the class board. Children will love matching the valentines to the correct classmates.

## "BUCKLE UP!" VALENTINE

A thoughtful gift for Mom and Dad on Valentine's Day that is a loving reminder. Have each student write the words "Buckle Up! I Love You!" on a simple valentine and place it on the dashboard of the family car.

## MAGAZINE VALENTINES

Ask students to look through old magazines and find pictures that might make comical valentines. Have them glue their pictures to a paper heart and write a valentine greeting that expresses the picture. Examples might be: "I've gone "nuts" over you!" (The picture might be a can of almonds or peanuts.) Or, "I'd be in a real "pickle" without a valentine like you!" (The picture would be a jar of pickles.) Display the valentines on the class board and ask students to vote for the most clever.

## HEART AND ARROW GAME

Draw a big heart on the chalkboard and divide the class into two or three teams. Have each child try to draw an arrow through the center of the heart while blind-folded. Give a score of "5" for each arrow that passes through the heart and "3" points for arrows that touch the heart. The team with the most points wins!

# Valentine Activities!

## FAMOUS VALENTINES

Ask your students to think of a famous person from which they would most like to receive a valentine. Would they like to send this person a valentine?

Provide a variety of colorful paper and pens, paper doilies, glitter, etc. and ask the students to make a valentine for their famous person. The valentines can then be displayed on the class board complete with a paper written by each student on the reasons they chose this particular person to be their valentine.

## FRUITY VALENTINES

Encourage your students to stay away from candy by making fruit leather hearts.

Place fresh or canned fruit in a blender and puree. Place the mixture in a sauce pan and simmer until thick. Cover a cookie sheet with plastic wrap and spread on the mixture about 1/4 inch thick. Place it in a 130 degree oven for 4 to 8 hours. When leathery, cut it into heart shapes and enjoy!

## "LOVELY" SYMBOLS

Brainstorm with your students on a list of Valentine Day's symbols. Ask them each to choose a symbol to research and tell why it is traditionally used to represent the holiday. Here are some suggestions:

| | |
|---|---|
| Hearts | Flowers |
| Cupid | Birds |
| Lace | Candy |

You may also like to have the students research the legend of Saint Valentine or find out how Valentine's Day is celebrated in other countries.

## VALENTINE BUTTON COVERS

Have students make valentines they can wear home or give away! Cut hearts from colorful pieces of felt about two inches square. Cut a slit in the center of each heart the size of a button hole. Students can draw faces or write valentine messages on the hearts with colored markers. Googly eyes can be glued in place for a truly goofy faced button cover.

## VALENTINE TELEGRAM

Ask students to comprise a valentine by using the letters, V-A-L-E-N-T-I-N-E. Give them a few minutes to write the message and then ask them to read their telegrams aloud.

# Love Knot

A long forgotten symbol of Valentine's Day is the "Love Knot." The Love Knot consists of graceful loops and bends that have no beginning and no end. Centuries ago, people would write loving messages on the endless loops and then give the knot to their sweetheart. The recipient would turn the knot to read the message.

Ask your students to write original valentine messages within the loops of this Love Knot or have them design their own Love Knot.

# Valentine Booklet

Name

Be My Valentine!

# Message Heart

Encourage students to write clever valentine poems or riddles on this valentine heart pattern.

Cut the hearts from red or pink construction paper and display them on the class bulletin board.

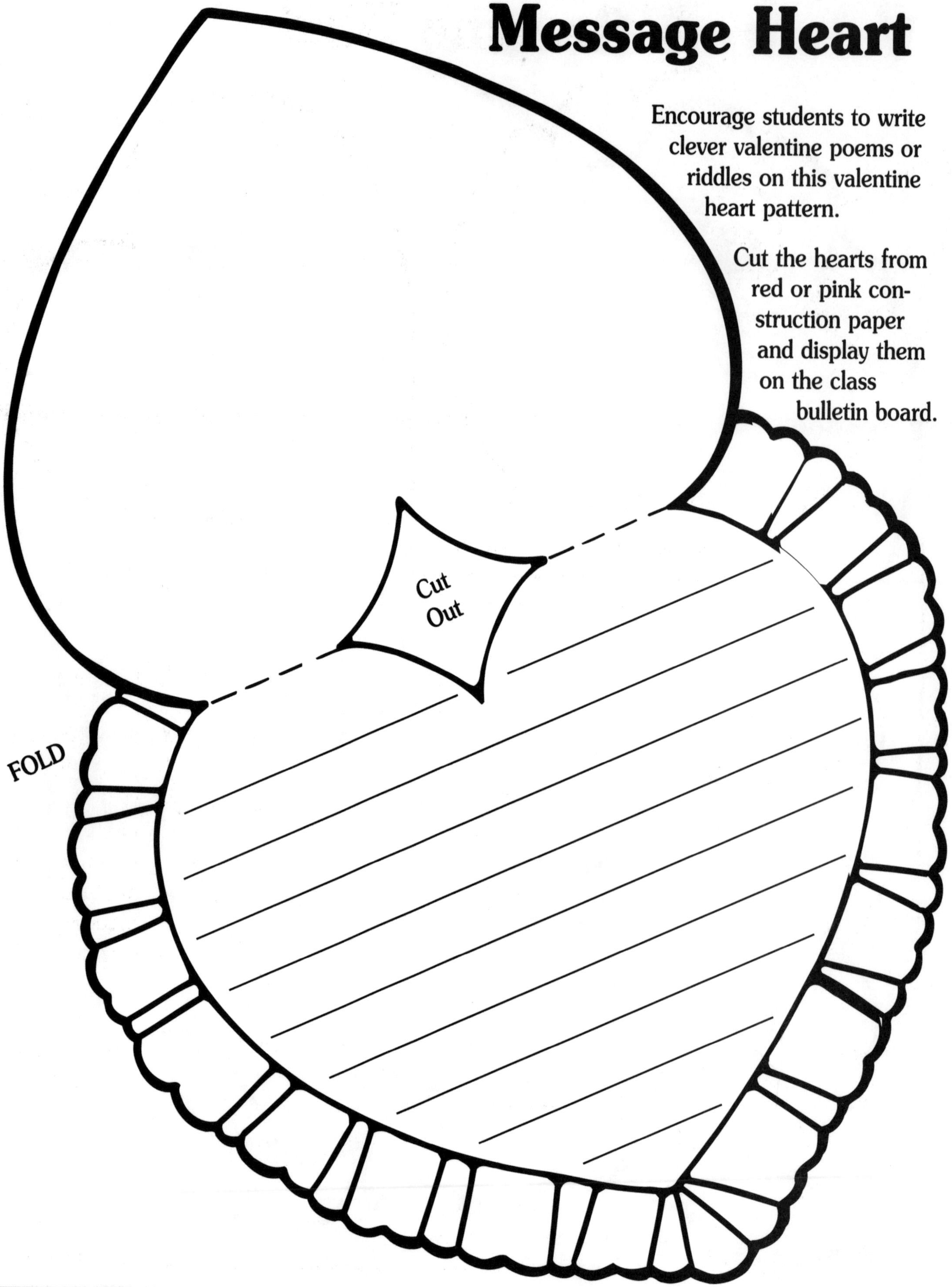

Cut Out

FOLD

# Valentine Bird

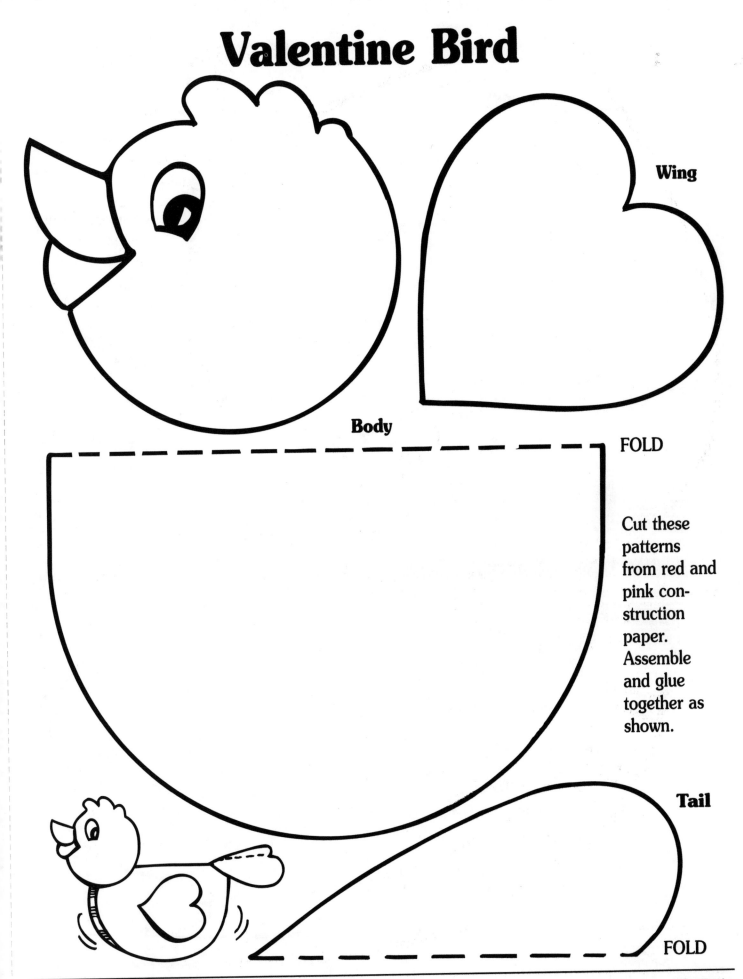

**Wing**

**Body**

FOLD

Cut these patterns from red and pink construction paper. Assemble and glue together as shown.

**Tail**

FOLD

Make a "Valentine Delivery Truck" envelope from a folded sheet of construction paper. Display the trucks on the board and have students place Valentines inside.

VALENTINE DELIVERY

Name

# Valentine Rhyming Words!

Write as many rhyming words as possible to the these Valentine words. Choose several rhyming words and use them in a Valentine's Day poem to a friend.

*Life is so cool when you do well in school!*

**blue** _____

_____

**sweet** _____

_____

**day** _____

_____

**red** _____

_____

**love** _____

_____

**see** _____

_____

**mine** _____

_____

# Cupid Wheel

Cut
Out

Cut
Out

Copy the "Cupid Wheel" onto heavy index paper. Color, cut out and assemble with brass fasteners. Cut out the two boxes, as shown.

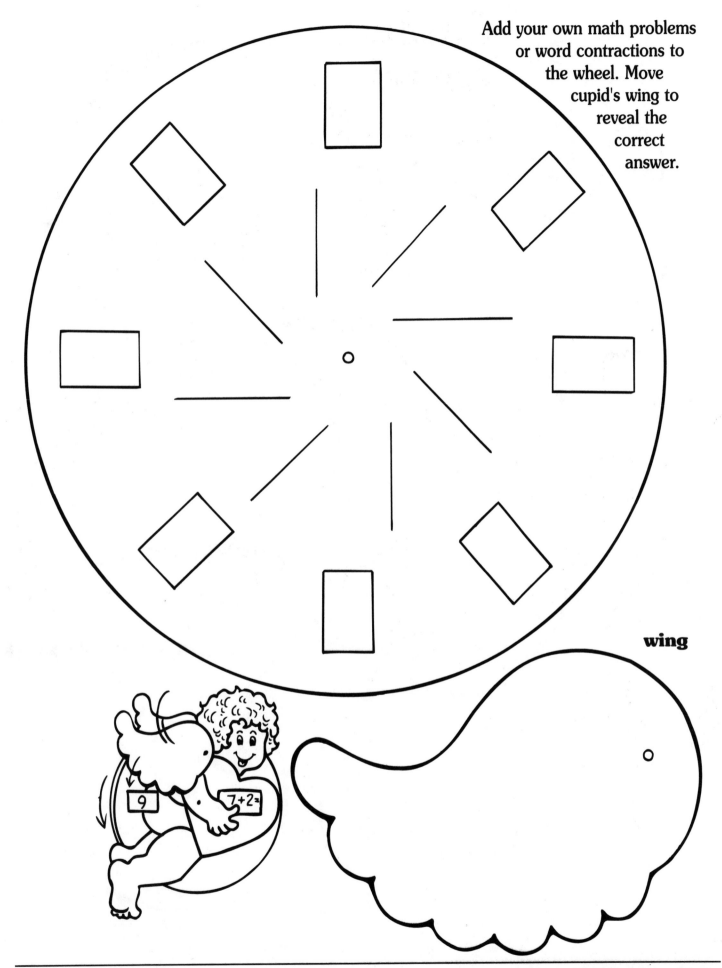

Add your own math problems or word contractions to the wheel. Move cupid's wing to reveal the correct answer.

**wing**

# Cupid Pattern

Name

Use this pattern to create a
valentine bulletin board.

Attach this cap pattern to a paper headband and award it to students for good behavior or completed assignments.

# Valentine Mail Carrier Cap

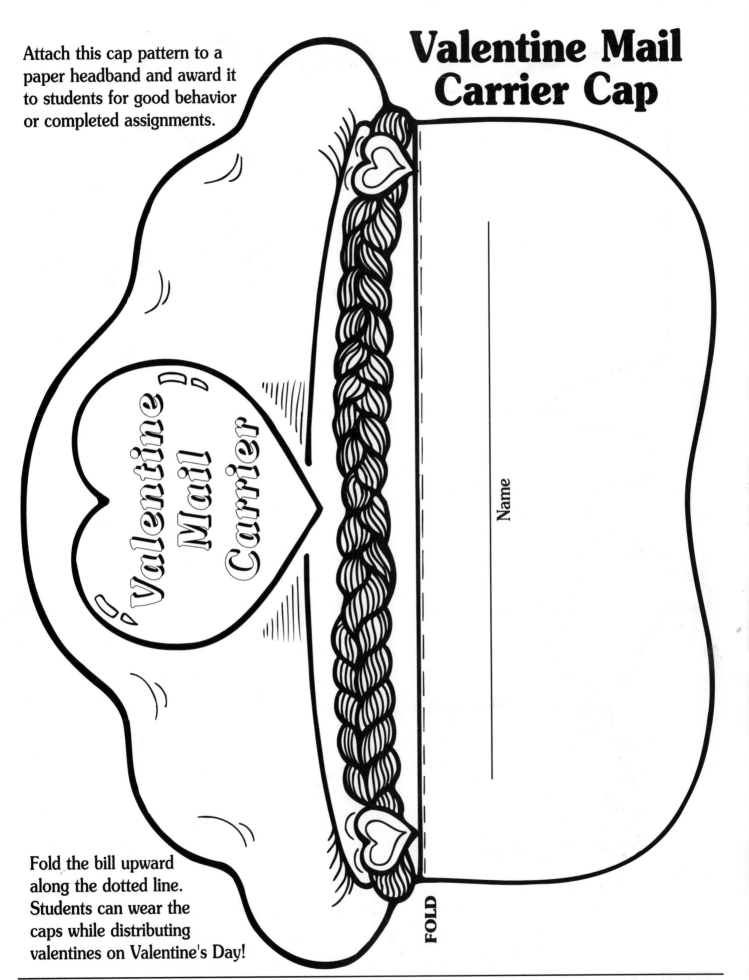

Valentine Mail Carrier

Name

FOLD

Fold the bill upward along the dotted line. Students can wear the caps while distributing valentines on Valentine's Day!

# Heart Pattern

Review math facts, contractions or write secret valentine messages using the patterns on these pages.

can   can't   not

_____

_____

_____

_____

_____

_____

_____

_____

○

# Opening Heart

Cut the two heart halves and the heart on the previous page from construction paper. Assemble as shown with a brass fastener.

# Valentine Crafts!

## ANIMAL LETTER BOXES

Children can make cute animal letter boxes to hold their valentines from discounted tissue boxes. Cover the boxes with construction paper and use paper plates for the animals' heads. Cut ears and tails from paper and glue in place. Pipe cleaner whiskers can also be added.

## "BE MY VALENTINE" CROWN

Cut several two-inch strips of red, white and pink construction paper. Staple one strip together to fit around a child's head. Staple either four or six strips of paper to the inside of the headband. Gather the strips together at the top and pull them toward the center, stapling them in place. Add a cut paper heart to the top of the crown.

(Valentine sayings can be written on the strips of paper before making the crown.)

Children will love parading their colorful crowns through the school halls.

# Teeth for Keeps!

# Dental Health!

February is Dental Health Month! Use this opportunity to instruct and encourage your students on the importance of taking care of their teeth.

In some cases, you may wish to set up a schedule for your students to brush their teeth at school. A local dentist may donate toothbrushes and toothpaste for the students' use. Provide each student with a daily brushing log for them to record those times they brush their teeth.

Here are a few suggested dental health activities to promote and inspire youngsters to brush regularly.

## TEETH, TEETH, TEETH

As a home assignment, ask each student to stand in front of the bathroom mirror and count their exact number of teeth. Have them write the number on a slip of paper. During class the next day, tally the number of teeth in the whole class and keep secret the number of teeth for the class members. The person with the closest guess could win a new toothbrush!

## THE TOOTH FAIRY

Encourage students to write imaginative stories using the tooth fairy as the main character. Students might like to speculate on what she does with all the teeth she finds, or where she lives.

Children may also like to write letters to the tooth fairy. Collect all the letters and then distribute them to older students who will write back creative responses.

## TOOTH SCIENCE

Demonstrate to your students how acids eat away the enamel on our teeth with this simple experiment. Place a raw egg in a clear glass of vinegar overnight. Ask students to speculate on what will happen. In the morning, you will see that the vinegar has slowly softened the shell in the same way acid softens tooth enamel. Explain to the children that when the enamel on our teeth is weakened, we get a toothache and a cavity.

## HOMEMADE TOOTHPASTE

Inspire your students to brush their teeth by making your own toothpaste. It's easy to make!

For every child in class, mix 1 tablespoon baking soda and a drop of peppermint flavoring. Add more drops if the mixture fails to make a paste. Spoon the paste onto each student's tooth brush. Hold a discussion as to which tastes better, homemade or store-bought toothpaste.

# Dental Health!

## TYPES OF TEETH

There are four different types of teeth that help perform different jobs. They are:

INCISORS - Located in the front of the mouth, these eight teeth have sharp, chisel-shaped crowns that cut food.

CUSPIDS - There is one cuspid next to each lateral incisor. Cuspids are pointed to help tear food.

BICUSPIDS - There are four pairs of bicuspids located next to the cuspids. They tear and crush our food.

MOLARS - There are four sets of three molars located at the back of our mouths. They help us by grinding our food.

Ask the students to try to locate the various teeth in their own mouths. By age 13 or so, children should have a full set of permanent teeth.

## TEETH IMPRINTS

Children will love this activity that allows them to thoroughly inspect their own teeth alignments.

Give each student a slice of American Cheese. Ask them to place the slice between their teeth and bite down gently. (Make sure you instruct them not to bite through the cheese.) Now, have them inspect their bite.

Do all of their teeth seem straight? Do the upper teeth fit inside the lower teeth? Does the imprint show any missing teeth? Ask them to measure the width of the arch.

## PARTS OF THE TEETH

Teeth provide three basic functions for the human body; Chewing provides the starting point of digestion, They help us speak properly and, finally, teeth add to our personal appearance.

It is also important that students know the different parts of their teeth. Ask your students to review the following:

CROWN - The part of teeth that we see.
ENAMEL - The hard, white outer covering of each tooth.
ROOT - The part of the tooth that is anchored in the gum.
DENTIN - A bone-like tissue inside the tooth.
PULP - The soft center of each tooth that houses the nerves and blood vessels.

## LOST TEETH

Display a large paper tooth on the class board. As children lose their teeth, write their names on the tooth. Keep a supply of small plastic bags for children to carry home the teeth they lose at school.

## TOOTH POEMS

Have children write short poems about brushing their teeth. Ask them to copy their poems onto a paper tooth. The poems can then be taken home and mounted on the bathroom mirror as a reminder to brush first thing in the morning and last thing at night.

**Toothy Puppet**

Cut this tooth puppet from white construction paper.

Glue both pieces to a small paper lunch bag.

# Lost Tooth Envelope

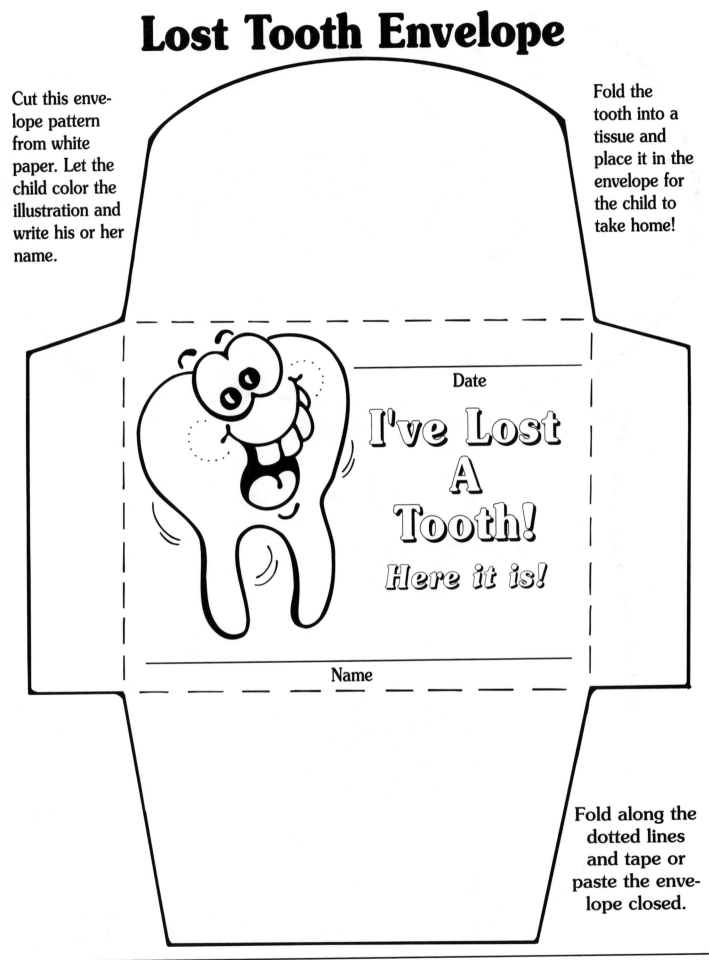

Cut this envelope pattern from white paper. Let the child color the illustration and write his or her name.

Fold the tooth into a tissue and place it in the envelope for the child to take home!

Date

## I've Lost A Tooth!
### Here it is!

Name

Fold along the dotted lines and tape or paste the envelope closed.

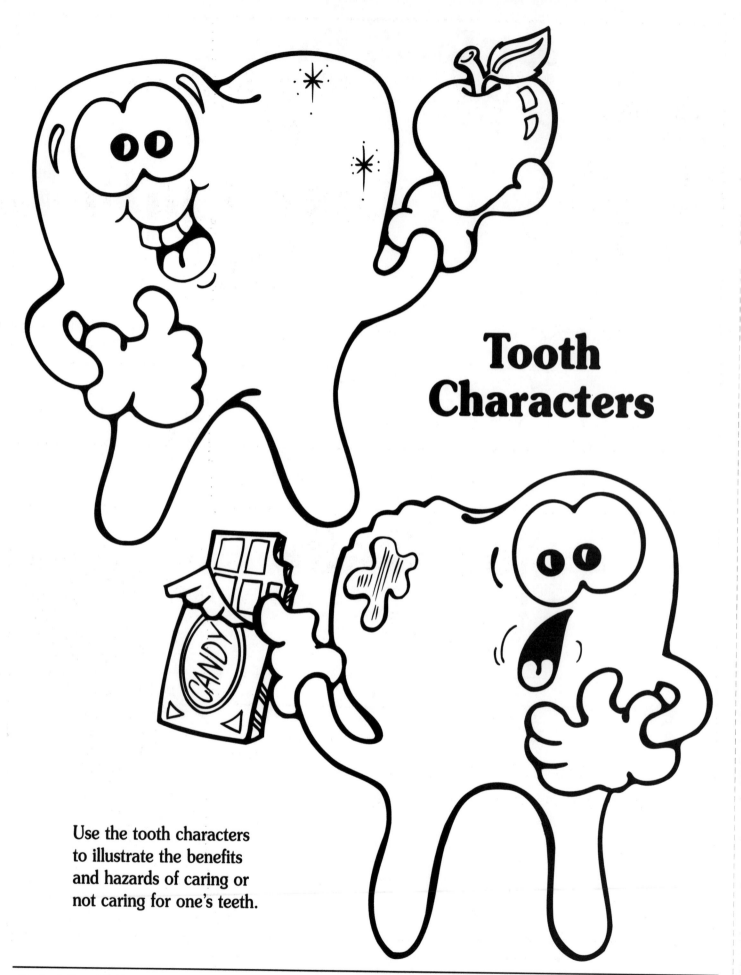

# Tooth
# Characters

Use the tooth characters
to illustrate the benefits
and hazards of caring or
not caring for one's teeth.

# I'm a member of the Lost Tooth Club

_____

Name

_____          _____

Teacher                                          Date

---

# Terrific Teeth Award

_____

Name

## has demonstrated good brushing techniques!

_____

Date

_____

Teacher

# Parts of a Tooth

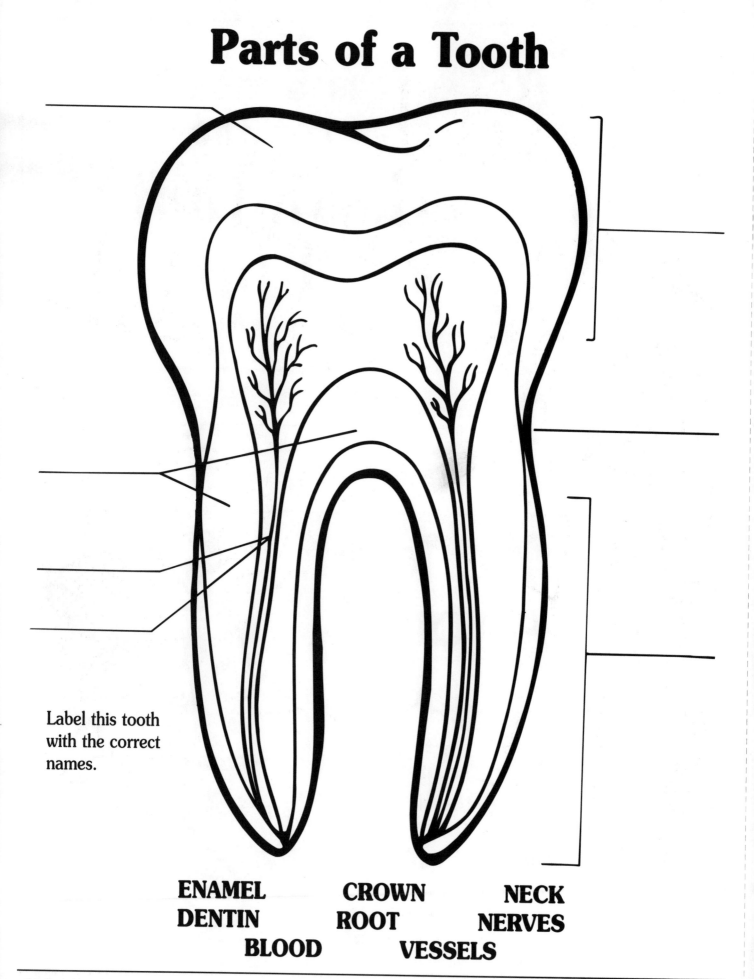

Label this tooth with the correct names.

**ENAMEL**
**DENTIN**
**BLOOD**
**CROWN**
**ROOT**
**VESSELS**
**NECK**
**NERVES**

My Smile Book!

_____
Name

# My Brushing Supplies

**The first thing I need to do is check my supplies!**

☐ **Toothbrush is in good shape and ready to use!**

☐ **Toothbrush is worn out!**
(Ask your parent to buy you a new one.)

☐ **I have fluoride toothpaste!**

☐ **I need to ask a parent to buy me some fluoride toothpaste!**

☐ **I have dental floss!**

☐ **I need to get some dental floss!**

# How Many Teeth?

**Most small children have 20 teeth. When these teeth are lost, they are replaced with 32 permanent teeth.**

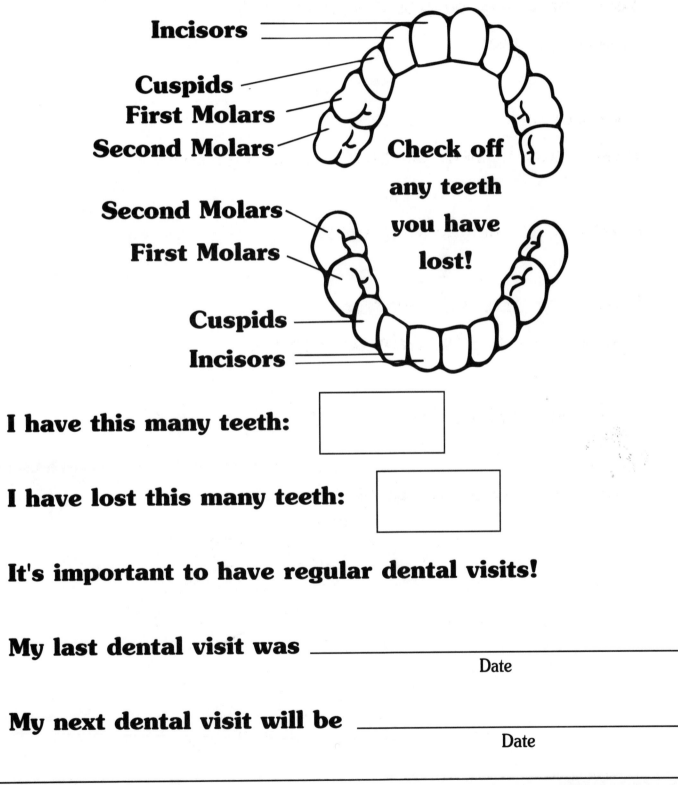

Incisors

Cuspids

First Molars

Second Molars

Check off any teeth you have lost!

Second Molars

First Molars

Cuspids

Incisors

**I have this many teeth:**

**I have lost this many teeth:**

**It's important to have regular dental visits!**

**My last dental visit was** _____
Date

**My next dental visit will be** _____
Date

# Learn to Brush Correctly!

Brush your teeth at a 45° angle with the bristles of the toothbrush toward the gums. Gently massage the gums and roll the brush toward the edge of each tooth.

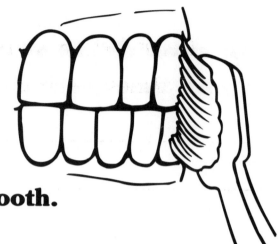

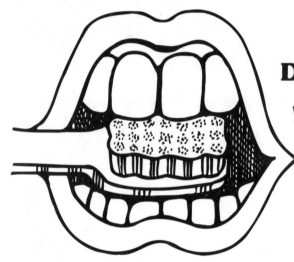

Don't forget to brush the back of your teeth. Use the same stroke, making sure the bristles go between each tooth.

It's probably best to use fluoride toothpaste to help prevent tooth decay.

Here are some other things I can do to prevent tooth decay.

1._____

2._____

3._____

4._____

# My Brushing Record

## I will brush at these times each day:

_____

_____

_____

| Sun | | Mon | | Tues | | Wed | | Thurs | | Fri | | Sat | |
|------|------|------|------|------|------|------|------|------|------|------|------|------|------|
| Brush | Floss | Brush | Floss | Brush | Floss | Brush | Floss | Brush | Floss | Brush | Floss | Brush | Floss |
| | | | | | | | | | | | | | |
| | | | | | | | | | | | | | |
| | | | | | | | | | | | | | |
| Brush | Floss | Brush | Floss | Brush | Floss | Brush | Floss | Brush | Floss | Brush | Floss | Brush | Floss |
| | | | | | | | | | | | | | |
| | | | | | | | | | | | | | |
| | | | | | | | | | | | | | |
| Brush | Floss | Brush | Floss | Brush | Floss | Brush | Floss | Brush | Floss | Brush | Floss | Brush | Floss |
| | | | | | | | | | | | | | |
| | | | | | | | | | | | | | |
| | | | | | | | | | | | | | |
| Brush | Floss | Brush | Floss | Brush | Floss | Brush | Floss | Brush | Floss | Brush | Floss | Brush | Floss |
| | | | | | | | | | | | | | |
| | | | | | | | | | | | | | |
| | | | | | | | | | | | | | |
| Brush | Floss | Brush | Floss | Brush | Floss | Brush | Floss | Brush | Floss | Brush | Floss | Brush | Floss |
| | | | | | | | | | | | | | |
| | | | | | | | | | | | | | |
| | | | | | | | | | | | | | |

## Color in each area of the chart when you brush and/or floss your teeth.

# Learn to Floss

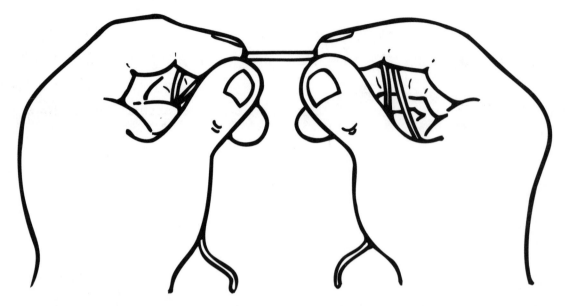

Tear off a piece of dental floss about 16 inches long. Hold the floss between your thumbs and forefingers as shown.

Work the floss between the teeth and gently move it up and down. Be careful not to miss any teeth!

Check the statements below that help to keep your teeth healthy.

- ☐ Visit the dentist
- ☐ Eat too much candy
- ☐ Eat fruits & vegetables
- ☐ Forget to brush
- ☐ Floss regularly

- ☐ Drink milk
- ☐ Drink soda pop
- ☐ Brush after meals
- ☐ Drink plenty of water
- ☐ Never see a dentist

# My Smile!

Here's a picture of myself and my smile!

This is what I've learned about caring for my teeth!

_____

_____

_____

_____

_____

_____

**I completed my booklet on** _____.

# Teeth for Keeps Visor

Copy this "Teeth for Keeps" visor onto sturdy index or construction paper. Children can do the coloring.

Punch holes at both ends and attach string elastic or mailing string. (With elastic, the students can easily remove the visors without retying.)

I will have Teeth for Keeps!

Name _____

# African-American Achievers

# Great African-Americans!

February is African-American Month in honor of the contributions and achievements made by African-Americans. Enlighten your students to the many cultural and historic contributions made by these great people. Assign each student one achiever to research. They may like to use these suggestions in their study.

## QUESTIONS TO ASK!

1. Is your African-American Achiever a hero? Why or why not?
2. What inspired your achiever to succeed?
3. How did your achiever's childhood differ from that of other children?
4. Did your achiever receive support or help from anyone? Who?
5. If you could interview your achiever, what would he or she say is their greatest accomplishment?

## TIME LINES

Ask students to create a time line noting the special events of a chosen African-American achiever's life. Have them begin with the date the achiever was born. Significant childhood events that helped form the achiever's character should also be noted. Make sure they also record the achiever's education, if they married and whether she or he had children. Have students continue the time line showing the various accomplishments their great person achieved throughout his or her life.

## IT'S ALL IN A NAME!

Instruct students to write poems or statements of fact using the letters in the name of a famous African-American. Tell them to make sure that each line accurately portrays their achiever's life. Here is an example using the name of Rosa Parks.

**P**     Picked crops on a plantation as a child
**A**     Appreciated and excelled in school
**R**     Refused to sit at the back of the bus
**K**     Ku Klux Klan could not defeat her
**S**     Segregation was stopped with the help of Rosa Parks

## EARNED AWARDS

Have students select a specific African-American achiever that has been recognized by earning a specific award. Ask them to research the award and the organization that gives it. Tell the students to find out how the recipients are selected and to list other persons that have received the honor.

## LIST OF ACCOMPLISHMENTS

Have students select one great African-American achiever and comprise a list of his or her accomplishments and facts without mentioning the achiever's name. Post the lists on the class board and have all students guess the identities. Award those students with the most correct answers with a special treat.

GREAT ACHIEVER!

_____

_____

for the grand accomplishment of

_____

_____

_____

_____

**Trophy Pattern**

_____

_____

# African-American Achievers Wheel

Create an informative game by matching the famous African Americans to their cultural contribution and/or achievement.

You may want to use these patterns to create a bulletin board display. Have children select one person to research. When completed, mount papers around the contribution wheel. Students can pin their famous person's name around the appropriate area of the wheel.

Cut this wheel from colored paper and paste it to the center of a large sheet of construction paper.

# African-American Achievers

### SPORTS
Jessie Owens
Jackie Robinson
Evelyn Ashford
Michael Jordan
Wilma Rudolph
Arthur Ashe

### HISTORY
Frederick Douglass
Mary McLeoud Bethune
Harriet Tubman
Crispus Attucks
Booker T. Washington
Matthew Hensen

### CIVIL RIGHTS
Correta Scott King
Ralph Abernathy
Sojourner Truth
Malcolm X
Rosa Parks
Martin Luther King Jr.

### LITERATURE
Maya Angelou
Alex Haley
Alice Walker
James Baldwin
Mildred Taylor
Langston Hughes

### SCIENCE/BUSINESS
Barry Gordy, Jr.
Oprah Winfrey
George Washington Carver
Daniel Hale Williams
Garrett Morgan
Benjamin Banneker

### MUSIC
Ray Charles
Louis Armstrong
Nat King Cole
Whitney Houston
Ella Fitzgerald
Duke Ellington

### ENTERTAINMENT
Bill Cosby
Spike Lee
Whoopi Goldberg
Sidney Poitier
James Earl Jones
Josephine Baker

### GOVERNMENT
Colin Powell
Thurgood Marshal
Shirley Chisholm
Ron Brown
L. Douglas Wilder
Carol Mosely-Braun

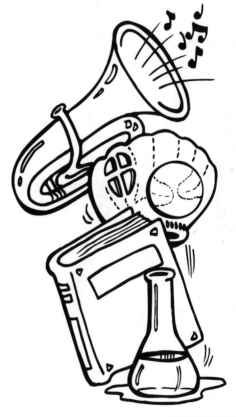

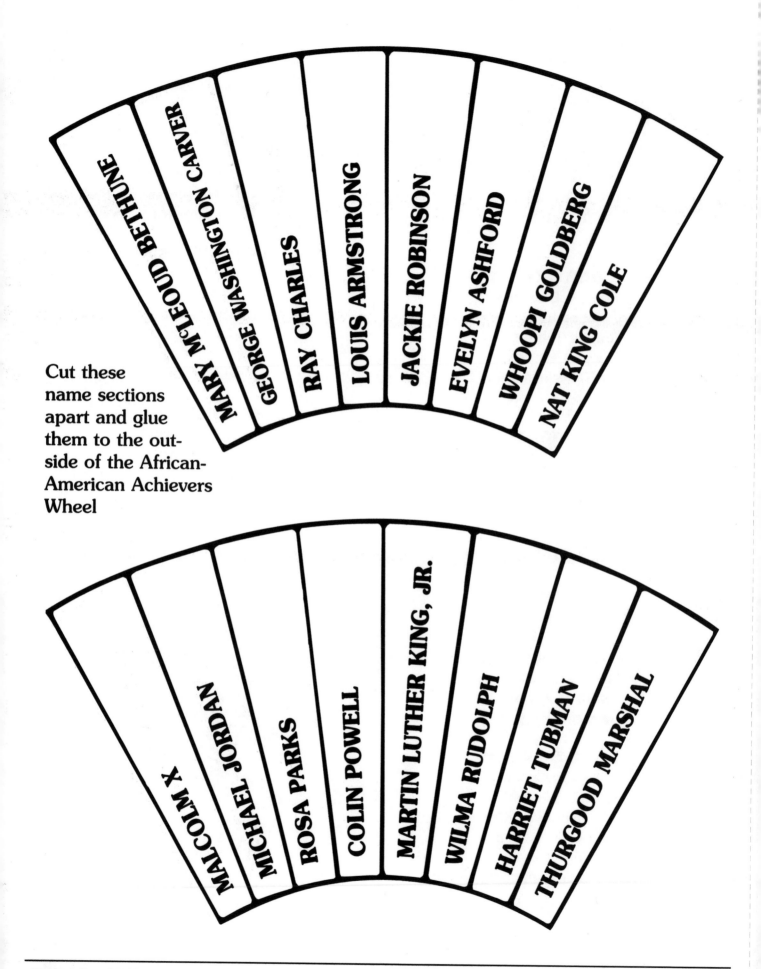

Cut these name sections apart and glue them to the outside of the African-American Achievers Wheel

MARY McLEOUD BETHUNE

GEORGE WASHINGTON CARVER

RAY CHARLES

LOUIS ARMSTRONG

JACKIE ROBINSON

EVELYN ASHFORD

WHOOPI GOLDBERG

NAT KING COLE

MALCOLM X

MICHAEL JORDAN

ROSA PARKS

COLIN POWELL

MARTIN LUTHER KING, JR.

WILMA RUDOLPH

HARRIET TUBMAN

THURGOOD MARSHAL

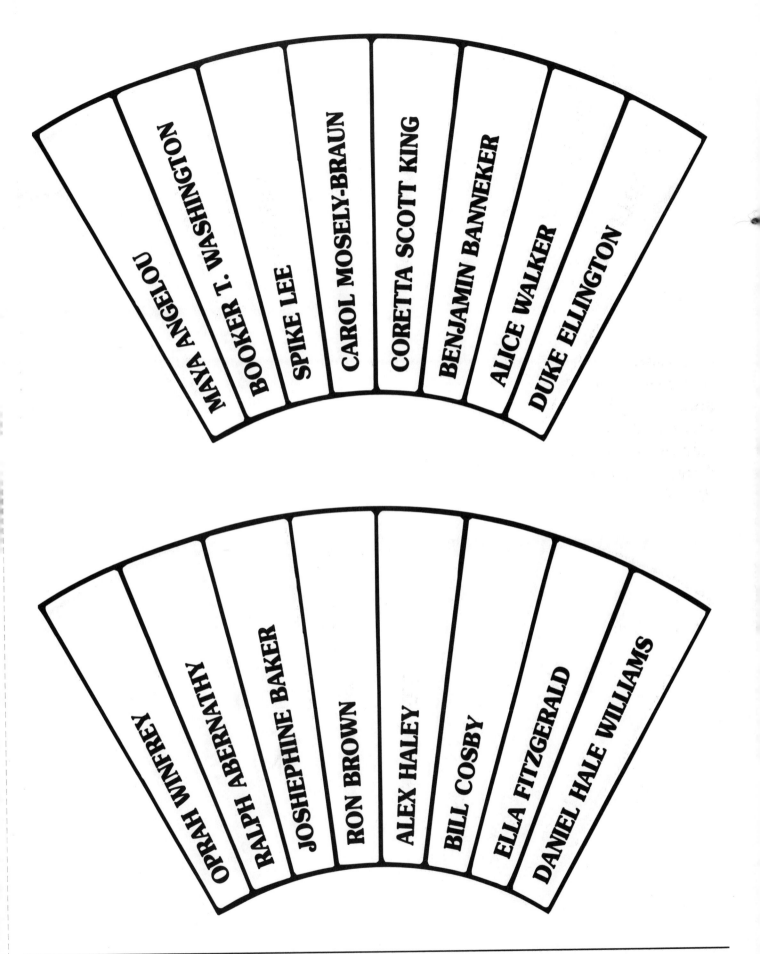

MAYA ANGELOU

BOOKER T. WASHINGTON

SPIKE LEE

CAROL MOSELY-BRAUN

CORETTA SCOTT KING

BENJAMIN BANNEKER

ALICE WALKER

DUKE ELLINGTON

OPRAH WINFREY

RALPH ABERNATHY

JOSHEPHINE BAKER

RON BROWN

ALEX HALEY

BILL COSBY

ELLA FITZGERALD

DANIEL HALE WILLIAMS

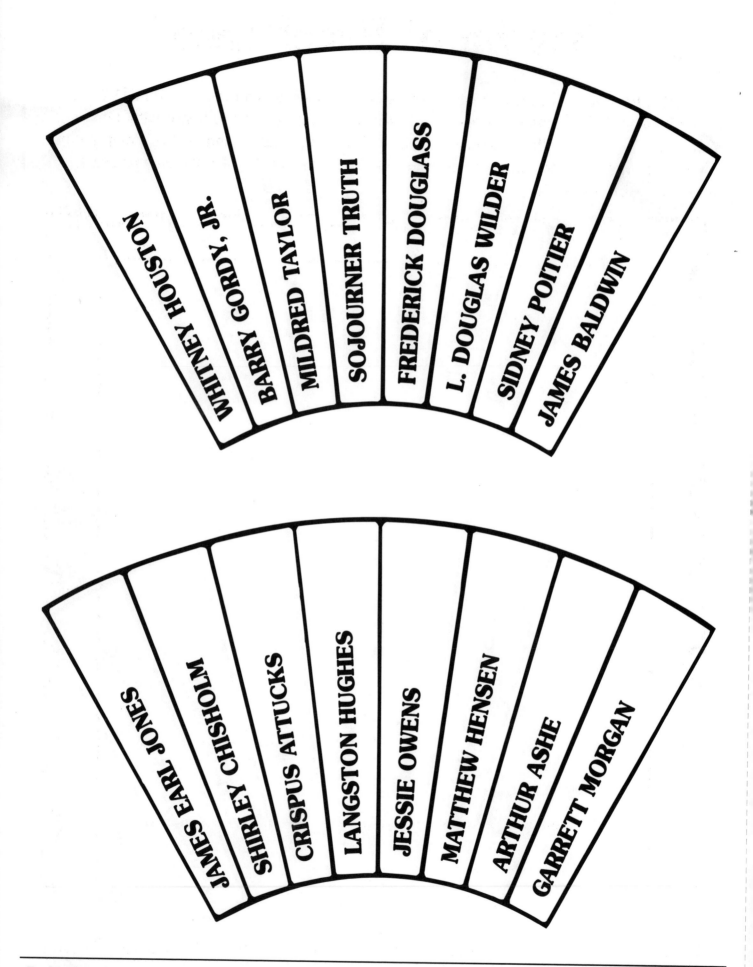

WHITNEY HOUSTON

BARRY GORDY, JR.

MILDRED TAYLOR

SOJOURNER TRUTH

FREDERICK DOUGLASS

L. DOUGLAS WILDER

SIDNEY POITIER

JAMES BALDWIN

JAMES EARL JONES

SHIRLEY CHISHOLM

CRISPUS ATTUCKS

LANGSTON HUGHES

JESSIE OWENS

MATTHEW HENSEN

ARTHUR ASHE

GARRETT MORGAN

# Stamp of Excellence

The first U.S. postage stamp to commemorate an African-American was issued in 1940 to honor Booker T. Washington. Have students select a famous person to honor with a commemorative stamp. Ask them to draw a picture of their honored person on this stamp pattern. Encourage them to write reports about his or her contributions. Display the stamps and reports on the class board.

Name

# My Report On An Accomplished African-American

**Name** _____

**Birthdate** _____ **Birth Place** _____
_____

**Early Years:** _____
_____
_____

**Overcoming Obstacles:** _____
_____
_____

**Major Accomplishments:** _____
_____
_____
_____

**Why this person is important!** _____
_____
_____
_____

# Heart Smart!

Beat

Heart Healthy

I'm Heart Smart!

HAPPY HEART!

# The Heart!

The heart is a powerful muscle which expands and con-tracts to pump blood to *every* part of the body. Everyone's heart is pear-shaped and about the size of a closed fist. As we grow, it will also grow in size. The heart is located in the middle of the chest, just behind the breastbone.

The heart is divided into two chambers. The left chamber, which is larger, pumps blood to the entire body. The right chamber, which is smaller, pumps blood only to the lungs.

Each of these chambers is divided into two smaller chambers. The upper sections are called *auricles* and the lower sections are called *ventricles*.

Blood vessels, called *arteries* carry the blood away from the heart. They expand and contract with the heart as the blood is pumped through the body.

From the arteries, the blood flows into *capillaries*, which are tiny tubes throughout the body. Anytime you have scraped your knee or pricked your finger, you have punctured a capillary.

The capillaries are then joined with tiny tubes called *veins* which unite with larger veins in the body to return the blood to the heart. This starts the blood flow all over again.

An adult's heart beats about 70 to 80 times a minute. It pumps over 2,500 gallons of blood each day.

Teach your kids to take their pulse. Show them how their pulse will increase with exercise and decrease with rest. Ask students to do the following:

1. Using the tips of your fingers, locate your pulse on either your wrist or neck.

2. Ask a friend to time you for 20 seconds while you count the number of times your heart beats.

3. How many times did your heart beat in 20 seconds? (Multiply this number by three to find out how many times your heart beats in a minute.)

4. Now, jog in place for a few minutes. This will speed up your heart rate.

5. Ask your friend to time you again. How many times did your heart beat in 20 seconds, this time? How many beats per minute?

Exercise makes your heart work faster and harder. It also helps your heart to become stronger and more efficient. There are many things you can do to keep your heart healthy and strong. It is important to get plenty of exercise, at least nine or ten hours of sleep every night, and eat a well-balanced diet.

# Healthy Heart Activities

## HEART BEATS

Explain to your students the function of the human heart including how the blood circulates through the body by way of veins. Emphasize that when the heart pumps, the veins stretch slightly causing a pulse. Instruct students to find their own pulses by pressing their middle fingers against the inside of their wrists or under the jaw on the neck.

You might also like to bring a stethoscope to class for your students to use to listen to each others' heartbeat. You can also make your own stethoscope by taping both ends of an 18 inch long, plastic tube to two small funnels. Instruct a student to hold one funnel to his or her own ear and place the other funnel against the left side of another student's chest. Ask the first student to count out loud each time he hears the heart beat. Now, ask the second student to jump up and down twenty times. Again, ask the first student to listen for and count the heart beats. Is the heart beat faster or slower? Tell students what when energy is expended by the body the heart works harder, causing the blood to pump faster. This creates the faster heart beat.

## HEART HEALTHY FOODS

With your students, list foods that are good for a healthy heart and those that are unhealthy. Stress the importance of eating a low fat diet full of fruits, vegetables, grains and proteins. Encourage students to look at the fat grams on favorite snacks such as potato chips and chocolate bars and discuss how unhealthy these foods are in our diets.

---

# Heart Smart!

_____
Name

knows that good nutrition, lots of exercise and plenty of sleep help to make a healthy heart and body.

_____
Date

_____
Teacher

---

# Parts of the Heart

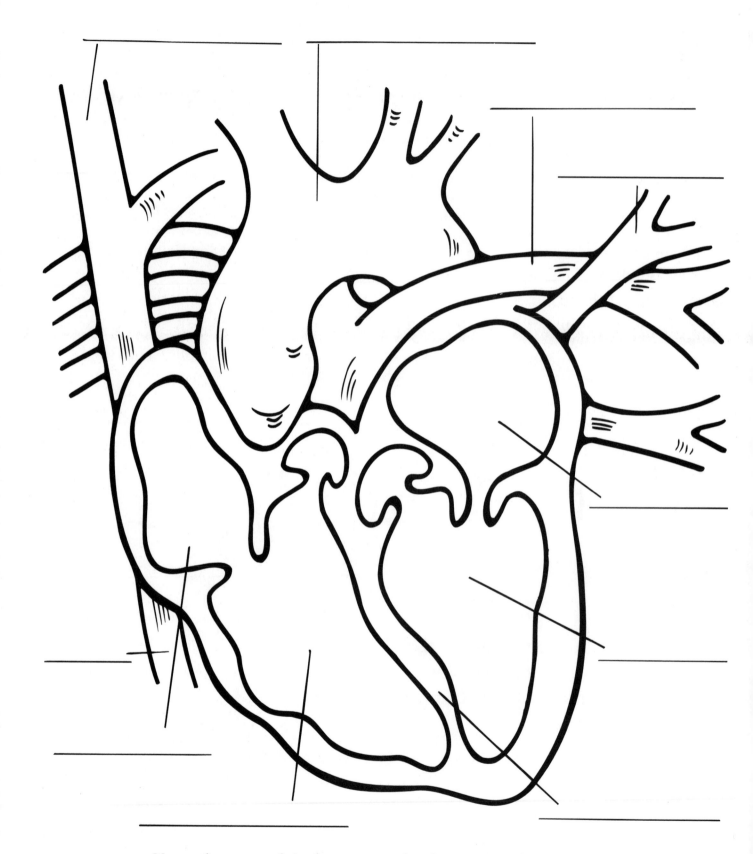

Name the parts of the heart using the diagram on the next page.

# Parts of the Heart

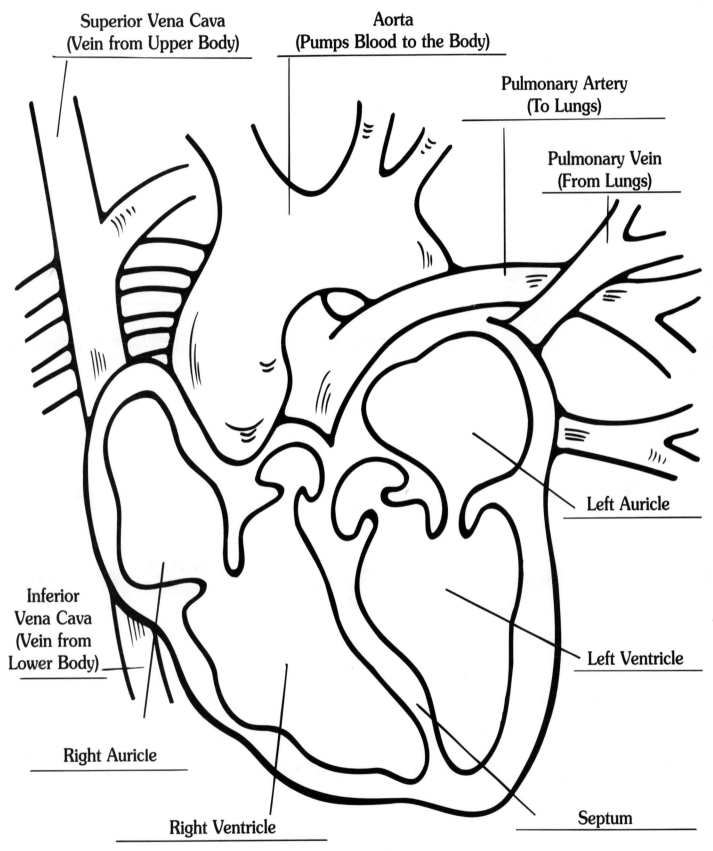

Superior Vena Cava
(Vein from Upper Body)

Aorta
(Pumps Blood to the Body)

Pulmonary Artery
(To Lungs)

Pulmonary Vein
(From Lungs)

Left Auricle

Left Ventricle

Inferior
Vena Cava
(Vein from
Lower Body)

Septum

Right Auricle

Right Ventricle

# Healthy Heart Mobile

**Heart Smart!**

_____

Name

Each student can make his or her own "Heart Smart Mobile" using these simple patterns. Cut the patterns from construction paper and assemble with thread or yarn, as shown on the next page.

You can also use this heart pattern to make "Heart Smart" Medallions. Attach yarn to each heart and hang the medallions around each child's neck.

Discuss with your class the different things they can do to have a healthy heart and body. You might ask students to list these things on the back of their mobile pieces. For example, list foods that make up a balanced diet, different activities that make the heart and body work hard and stay fit and the number of hours of sleep we all need each night to keep our bodies in the best possible health.

Cut Mr.
Heartbeat
patterns
from heavy
paper and
assemble with
brass fasteners.

# Mr. Heartbeat

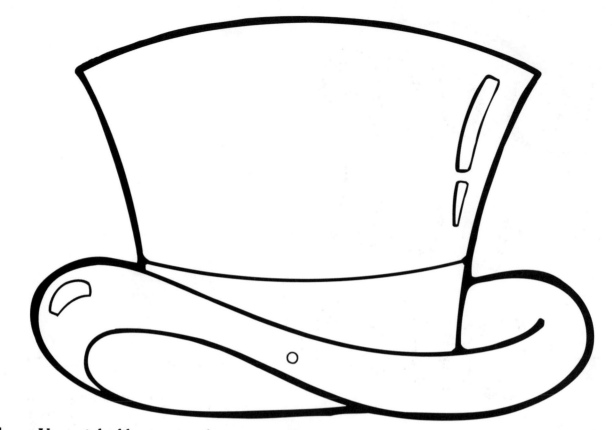

**Teachers:** You might like to award a pattern piece of Mr. Heartbeat for good behavior or completed assignments. Children can assemble the pieces when they have collected all six.

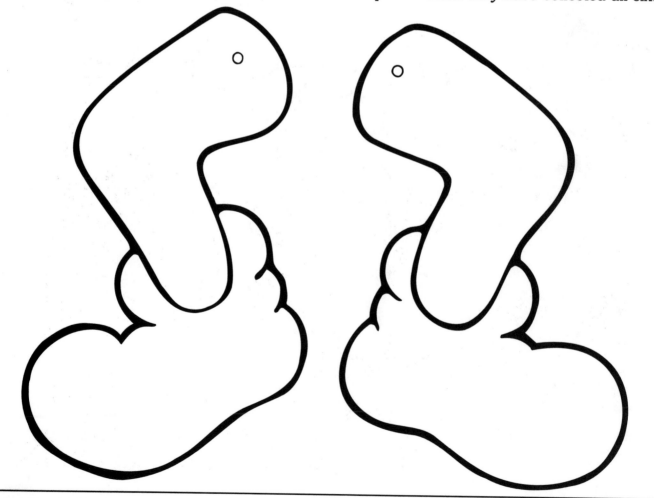

# Dogs and Cats!

# Dog and Cat Activities!

Use the theme of family pets to motivate students into learning responsibility and the qualities of being loving and caring. This subject can also be used to inspire students with creative writing assignments and math exercises.

## CAT AND DOG RULES

Cats and dogs deserve to be treated with patience, compassion and consideration for their needs. Ask your students to write a list of rules for caring for a family pet. The list may include some of the following:

1. Before bringing a pet home, make sure you have the time and ability to properly care for it.

2. Make sure that it has a dry, clean and quiet place to eat and sleep.

3. Make sure that it gets plenty of fresh water and a daily balanced diet.

4. Make sure your pet has proper veterinary care.

5. Teach your pet to be obedient. Reward your pet for good behavior. Never strike or hit your pet.

6. Make sure your pet's environment is safe. Pets should not be allowed to roam free and unsupervised.

7. Research and read about the special needs of your pet.

8. Love your pet. Make sure you spend time just loving your pet every day!

## CANINE SAYINGS

List some of these familiar sayings or words on the class board and ask your students to write creative stories or simply explain what they think they mean. It may be fun for the students to illustrate the phrases.

It's Raining Cats and Dogs
Let Sleeping Dogs Lie
You Can't Teach an Old Dog New Tricks
It's a Dog's Life
Hot Diggity Dog
Dog Day Afternoon
Fighting Like Cats and Dogs
Dog Days of Summer
Under Dog
Dog Paddle
Three Dog Night
You're in the Dog House
Dog Tags
Puppy Love
Dog Gone It
Dog Tired
Dog Eared
Pup Tent

# Dog and Cat Activities!

## DOGGIE BONES

Use a doggie bone pattern to teach alphabetical skills. Make several copies of bones from heavy white paper. Write one word you wish the student to alphabetize on each bone. Keep the bones in an empty dog biscuit box. Children can take all of the bones from the box and arrange them in alphabetical order.

You can also use doggie bone patterns to motivate creative writing assignments. Try some of these ideas:

The Dog That Loved Cats
How to Wash a Hundred Pound Dog
The Coward Watchdog
The Biggest Dog in the World
The Smallest Dog in the World
The Day My Dog Came to School
The Dog Whot Ate Too Many Dog
    Biscuits
The Dog That Chased Cars
The Dog That Couldn't Bark
The Dog Who Was Afraid of Cats

## CAT AND DOG GRAPHS

Students will enjoy this math activity that involves their family pets.

Instruct students to survey the members of their class and ask which children have one or more cats and dogs as pets. Have them record the color of each cat or dog whether it's male or female, color of eyes, long hair or short hair, etc.

On the class chalkboard, have students graph their findings. What is the most common color of the animals? Are there more males or females? What percentage wears collars? How many have green eyes?

Students will enjoy recording these interesting statistics and at the same time will learn about percentages and averages.

## DOG BISCUIT RECIPE

National Dog Week is usually the first week in September. Celebrate by having your students make dog biscuits to take home and give to their family canine!

2 cups biscuit mix
1/2 cup corn meal
1/4 cup vegetable shortening
1/3 cup grated yellow cheese
2/3 cup milk

Preheat the oven to 400°. Mix the biscuit mix and corn meal together. Add the shortening and cheese. Stir in the milk, mixing all ingredients together. Roll the dough onto a floured board and cut into small squares or use a cookie cutter. Place on a greased cookie sheet and bake about 15 minutes.

# Cat Paper Bag Puppet

# Dog Paper Bag Puppet

Cut these pattern pieces from construction paper and paste them to a small lunch bag to make each puppet.

# Be Kind to Animals! Award

presented to

_____

for

_____

_____

_____
Teacher

_____
Date

# Dog and Cat Finger Puppets!

Cut Out          Cut Out

Cut Out          Cut Out

# Accordion Doxie

Have students stretch this dog as long as they like by cutting a long strip of paper (4 inches wide) and folding it accordion style. Ask them to cut each doxie pattern from brown construction paper and paste the folded strip, as shown. Students can write vocabulary words, math facts, etc., on each fold of the doxie's body.

# Cat
# Booklet

FOLD

Name

# Dog Booklet

FOLD

Name

# A Pet of My Own!

______________________
Student's Name

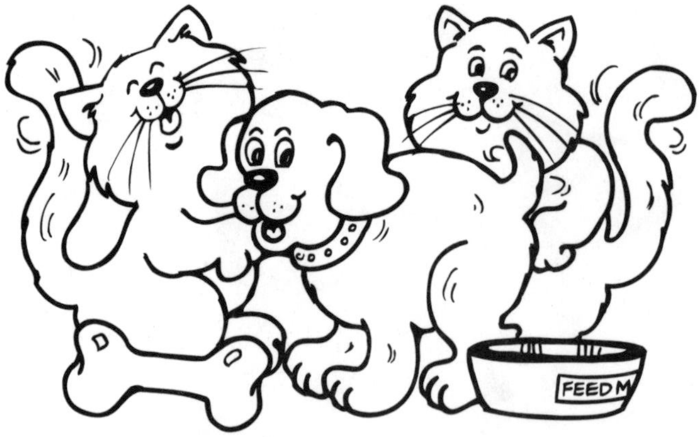


**My favorite pet is:**

______________________

______________________

**Color of my pet:**

______________________

**My pet will grow to be __________ inches tall/long.**

**My pet eats ______________________**

______________________

______________________

**I feed my pet ________ times a day.**

**It's important that pets are cared for properly.**

**Here are three special things my pet needs:**

**1.** ______________________

**2.** ______________________

**3.** ______________________

**The benefits of having this pet are ______________________**

______________________

______________________

**However, sometimes ______________________**

______________________

______________________

______________________

**(Teachers: Students can select a pet they own to write about or one they wish they had.)**

# Bulletin Boards and More!

LOVE is...

having Mommie tuck me in bed!

Spending the night at Grandmas!

being kind to animals!

cleaning my room without being asked!

Daddy reading me a story!

helping my dad with the dishes!

giving my sister a big hug!

helping my teacher in class!

# Bulletin Boards and More!

## TEETH FOR KEEPS

Display a large, toothy smile on the class bulletin board and surround it with suggestions for healthy teeth.

(The same big smile can also be used to display student-created jokes and riddles.)

## THE HEARTLAND

Ask each child to fold a large sheet of construction paper to form a pocket. Staple the sides together. Students can draw their own house designs or use the pattern on the next page. Display all of the houses on the class bulletin board, adding paths, roads, trees and clouds. Children will love filling the houses with special valentines on February 14th.

## HEARTS A FLUTTER!

Have each student cut out identical hearts from red, pink, purple or white construction paper. Ask them also to cut a long, narrow oval for the butterfly's body. The hearts become the butterfly's wings when they are pasted to the back of the body, as shown. Pipe cleaners can be added for antennae. To decorate, add small pieces of tissue paper, glitter, or sequins.

# Bulletin Boards and More!

## COOKIE PHONICS!

Display several paper cookie jars on the class board and label each one with a short or long vowel. Cut dozens of cookies from construction paper. Write one word that applies to the vowel sound on each cookie. Children pin the cookies to the appropriate cookie jars.

You may also want to give each student their own cookie jar to collect cookie awards!

## TERRIFIC TEETH

Let each child earn gold stars on his or her own paper tooth with this "Terrific Teeth!" bulletin board.

Award the stars for the following good dental habits:
- Brushing twice a day.
- Flossing twice a day.
- Seeing a dentist twice a year.
- Eating healthy foods.
- Staying away from sweets.

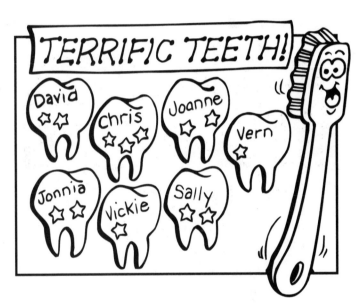

## TAKE HEART!

Make an extra large "Valentine" character using accordion folded strips of paper and six cut-paper hearts. Pin it on the class bulletin board and display good work papers with a "hearty" valentine saying.

Children will love making their own "Valentine" characters to take home.

# Bulletin Boards and More!

## TOP "TEN"

Cut ten circles from black construction paper and pin them to the bulletin board. (Use silver paper to make CDs.) Write the names and authors of ten favorite books on smaller circles of contrasting colors. Glue these to the center of each black circle to resemble a record label.

This idea can also be used for book reports!

## HAVE HEART!

Cut two extra large hearts from red butcher paper. Staple around the edges and stuff lightly with crumpled newspaper. Toilet tissue can be stapled in place for a ruffle. Display the heart on a bulletin board and surround it with good work papers or creative writing assignments about Valentine's Day!

## MATCHING PRESIDENTS

Display a silhouette or picture of both Lincoln and Washington on the class bulletin board. List their various accomplishments down the center of the board. Use colorful yarn to match each fact with the appropriate president.

# Cookie Jar Pattern

# Cookie Patterns

Make several copies of these cookie patterns. Try one of these activities with your students!

Write scrambled spelling words, mixed-up sentences, or story starter ideas on either pattern. Store the cookies in a real cookie jar or empty cookie box.

Draw chocolate chips on the cookies with a brown crayon or marker and ask young children to count the chips. This makes a cute bulletin board idea where children can pin the correct answer next to the appropriate cookie.

Name

**Tooth
Pattern**

# House Pattern

Name

# House Pattern

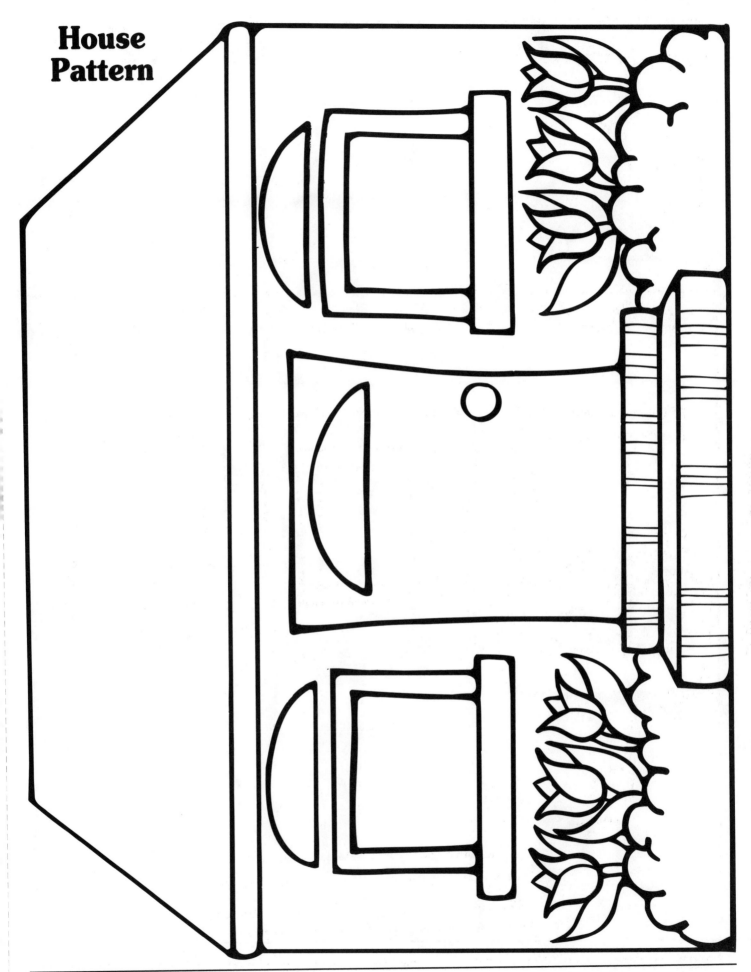

# Teacher's Friend Alphabet

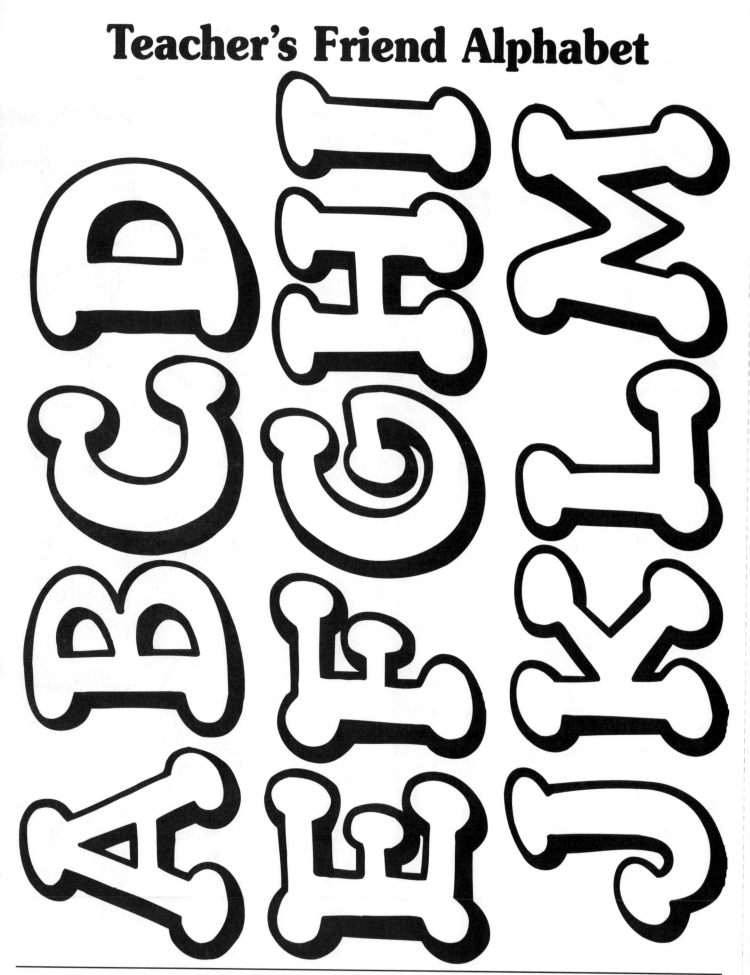

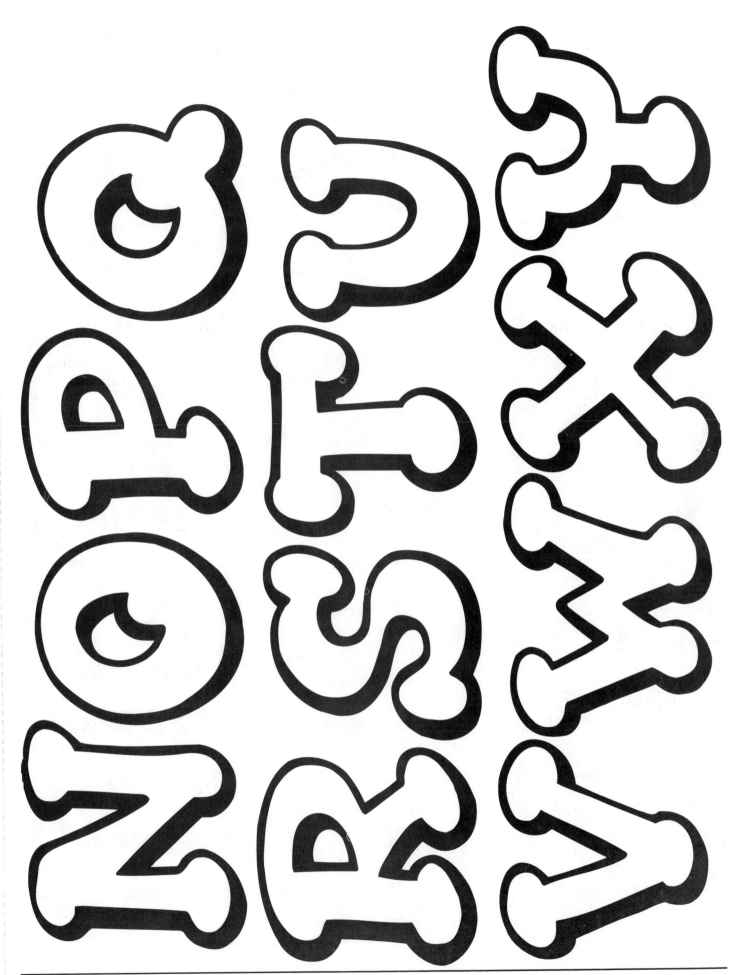

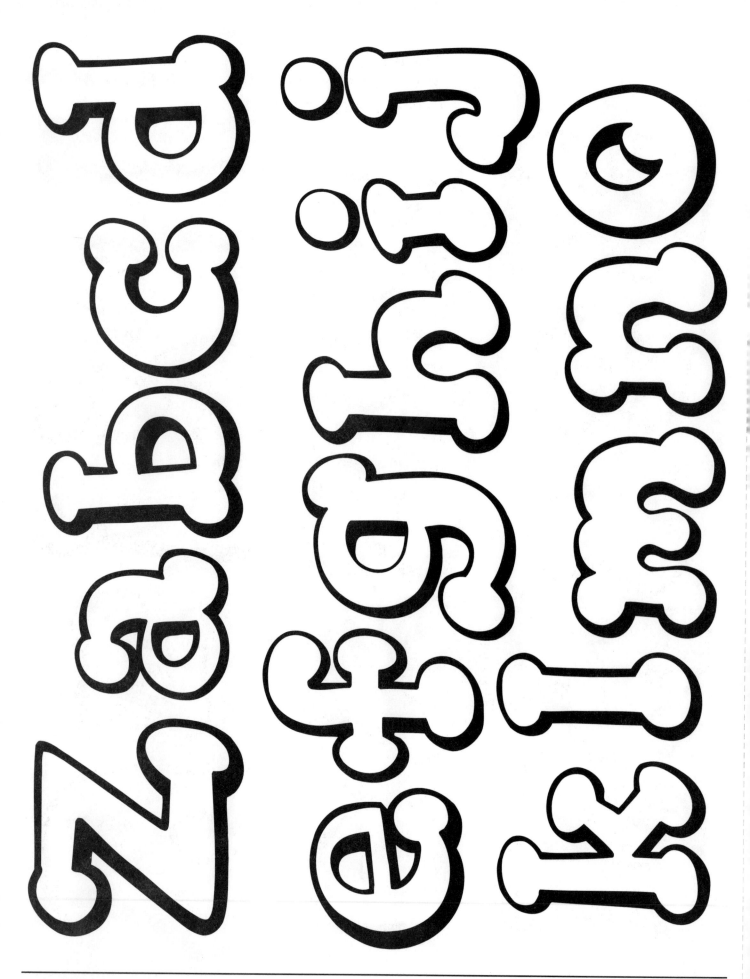

Teachers: Use these letters and numbers in a variety
of ways. Feel free to enlarge or reduce the size of the
characters for your classroom use.

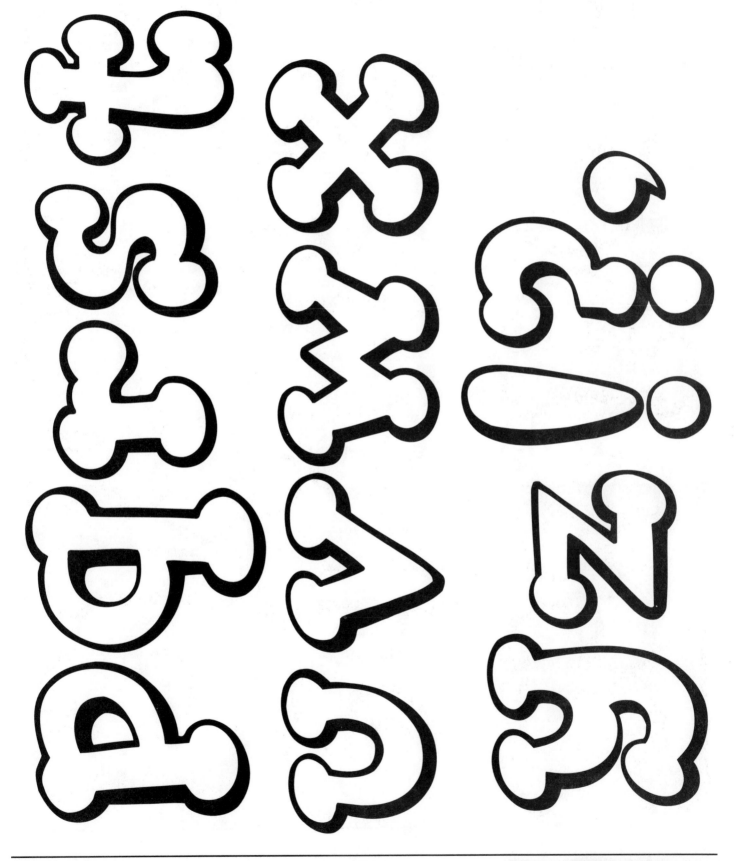

# Teacher's Friend Numbers

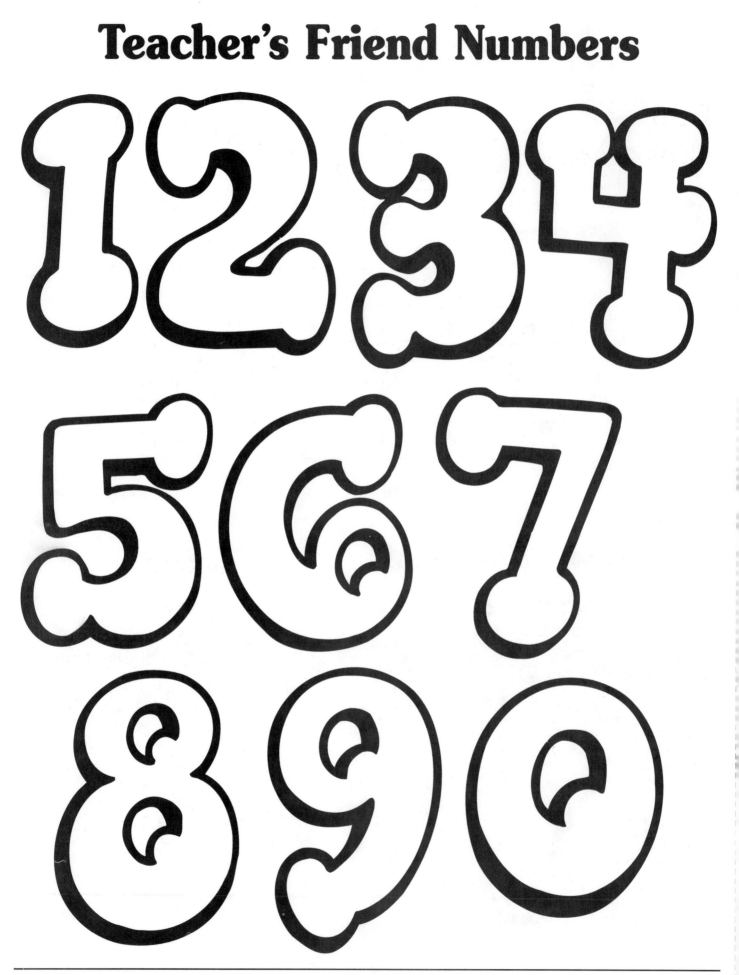

# Answer Key!

## February Crossword

ACTIVITY 1

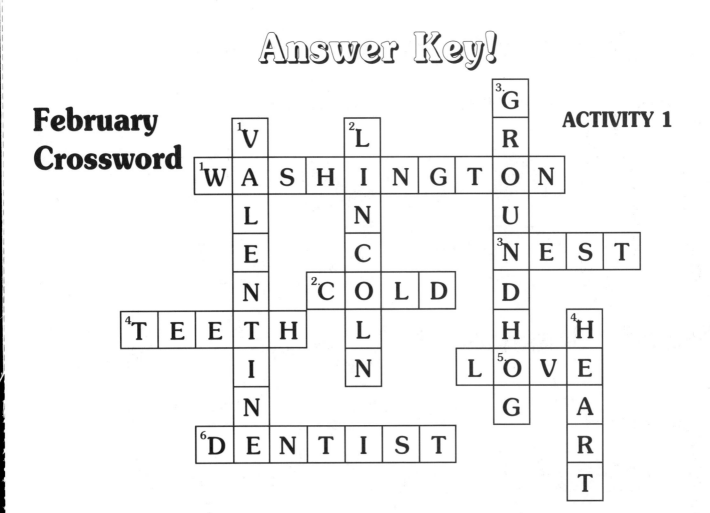

The crossword grid contains the following answers:

- 1 Across: WASHINGTON
- 2 Across: COLD
- 3 Across: NEST
- 4 Across: TEETH
- 5 Across: LOVE
- 6 Across: DENTIST
- 1 Down: VALENTINE
- 2 Down: LINCOLN
- 3 Down: GROUNDHOG
- 4 Down: HEART

## February Word Find!

### ACTIVITY 2

```
A Z X C D F V W A S H I N G T O N V D F T G
A X V S E R F B N M J K L O P T Y G H B W E
C D A R F G H J K C U P I D C V B N H Y I G
W C L T Y U I V D F G H Y R V B N M F S N Y
X V E V B L O V E G Y H R T Y U I K L H T J
C G N Y J K I U F R T E W Q X C V B H J E Y
A F T F B H G Y T N D A G K C X V H Y F R B
F T I F B H N J N M U R F G H J K L O D T U
G J N V G T Y H J U Y T C F D E S R T H Y U
S C E G R O U N D H O G V H Y T E W Q C H G
C B H Y U J M L S V B H Y U I O P L K J M G
S D C H E R R Y N J I K F D S W Q A C B G D
X V F T G B N M O U Y T R E W Q F G H J K L
A S H A D O W R W F G H B N M K J I U K L O
B N H J K L O I U J K M N B G L I N C O L N
S C V G Y H N M J K I U Y T G F R E D C V B
S C V G F E B R U A R Y G B N J U G R E W D
```

Circled words: WASHINGTON, CUPID, LOVE, VALENTINE, GROUNDHOG, CHERRY, SHADOW, SNOW, WINTER, HEART, LINCOLN, FEBRUARY

## ACTIVITY 3

### Groundhog Maze

# Answer Key!

## Washington Word Find!

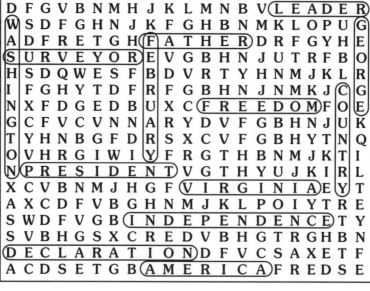

```
D F G V B N M H J K L M N B V L E A D E R
W S D F G H N J K F G H B N M K L O P U G
A D F R E T G H F A T H E R D R F G Y H E
S U R V E Y O R E V G B H N J U T R F B O
H S D Q W E S F B D V R T Y H N M J K L R
I F G H Y T D F R U F G B H N J N M K J G
N X F D G E D B U X C F R E E D O M F O E
G C F V C V N N A R Y D V F G B H N J U K
T Y H N B G F D A S X C V F G B H Y T N Q
O N V H R G I W I Y F R G T H B N M J K T I
N P R E S I D E N T V G T H Y U J K I R L
X C V B N M J H G F V I R G I N I A E Y T
A X C D F V B G H N M J K L P O I Y T R E
S W D F V G B I N D E P E N D E N C E T Y
S V B H G S X C R E D V B H G T R G H B N
D E C L A R A T I O N D F V C S A X E T F
A C D S E T G B A M E R I C A F R E D S E
```

**ACTIVITY 4**

## Valentine Crossword!

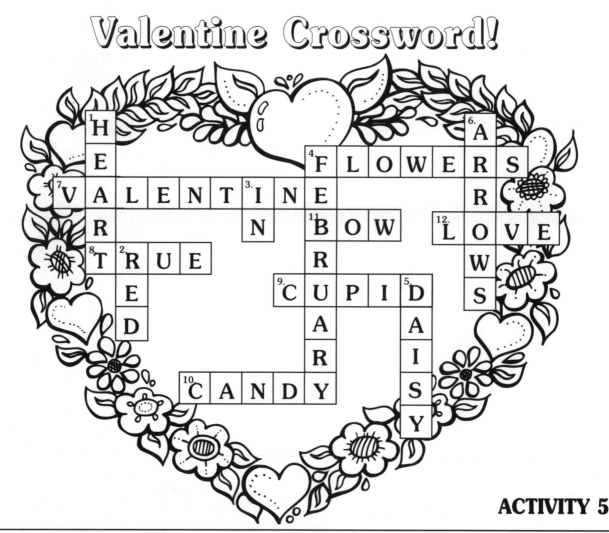

**ACTIVITY 5**

---